2-26-61 39-20270

ORIENTAL
ASSEMBLY

Camels belonging to T. E. LAWRENCE, January 1918

ORIENTAL ASSEMBLY

by

T. E. Lawrence

Edited by
A. W. LAWRENCE

*With Photographs by
the Author*

NEW YORK
E. P. DUTTON & CO. INC.
1940

PRINTED IN GREAT BRITAIN

FOREWORD

THIS volume comprises practically all the author's miscellaneous writings, with the exception of *Crusader Castles*. I hope that essay, already printed as a personal document in a limited edition, will eventually be reissued as a work of scholarship, with annotations and additional matter by several authorities. There remains nothing else which I intend to place before the general public.

A. W. L.

CONTENTS

vii

LIST OF ILLUSTRATIONS

ORIENTAL ASSEMBLY

THE WAR PHOTOGRAPHS

LIST OF ILLUSTRATIONS

xi

I

DIARY OF A JOURNEY ACROSS THE EUPHRATES

EDITOR'S NOTE

IN a letter from Jerablus, dated June 24, 1911, T. E. Lawrence told his mother of the British Museum's decision to cease work on the mound that covers the ancient city of Carchemish; the excavators were then to descend the Euphrates by boat and visit the site called Tell Ahmar. "After three days there I will walk across to Harran, up to Urfa, to Biredjik, and back to Aleppo by Tell Bashar and this place. This will be a walk of about a month, for there will be several days each in Harran and Urfa."

Another letter followed, from Tell Ahmar: "We have been here about four or five days working out a cuneiform inscription, photographing and squeezing things Hittite. Now it is all over, and to-day in the afternoon I am going off towards Urfa. The men here say it is best to go along the carriage road as far as Seruj (about 2 days) and then take another road. This route I may vary of course as I get later information." He was then in doubt whether to return through Aintab or Tell Bashar.

The objects of this journey were largely archæological. There was—in fact there still is—much work for a student of castles in this area. He had seen those at Urfa and Biredjik in 1909; but his time had then been extremely limited and his knowledge had since increased. Moreover, there were reported to be castles of note at Harran, Rum Kalaat and Aintab. Another motive was the search for engraved seal-stones of the local "Hittite" types; the Ashmolean Museum at Oxford owns the largest collection of them, mostly purchased from villagers through the various excavators of Carchemish; some were acquired on this occasion. (There is an illustrated catalogue by D. G. Hogarth.) And perhaps another incentive to this journey may be traced: it would lead to strange people and places.

The Diary occupies a block of centre pages in a small canvas-bound notebook, the rest of which contains personal memoranda (expense accounts and addresses), data on the ancient East, translations of Arabic fables, etc. Each day's happenings were described that evening and on the following morning. With the exception of an alteration in the initial date, the few corrections seem to have been inserted on reading through the day's entry immediately after its completion; there is no sign of any general revision. The wording changes character according to the writer's state of health, the punctuation varies correspondingly.

Probably he intended to rewrite the whole, for it would seem that he must have had a literary motive for the unusual exercise of keeping a diary and for persisting in so doing under such physical difficulties. In a conversation with Professor L. B. Namier, he once referred to having written something called *Seal-Hunting in Mesopotamia*. Search has been made through magazines of the years before the War, but in vain, and indeed the preservation of the Diary in its original form suggests that it was never published by its author. (It appeared after his death in a limited edition.)

The text as now printed is virtually an exact transcription of the pencil manuscript. To have removed all the inconsistencies and cleaned up the punctuation would have altered the effect without greatly improving the sense; and having to choose between two causes of annoyance we have preferred excessive fidelity to over-editing.

Some of the photographs mentioned in the Diary cannot be traced, while others, not mentioned in the text, were obviously taken on this journey.

Where necessary, I have added Notes at the end of each day's entry.

A. W. L.

DIARY OF A JOURNEY ACROSS THE EUPHRATES

ON a Wednesday about July 12 I left Tell Ahmar, and walked about an hour: then, feeling thirsty I went to some Kurdish tents, in which the villagers of some houses close by were staying, and got leben and barley bread; no money accepted.

Then walked on three hours till I came to the Khan, which was deserted: met a villager or two, however—one Shirkub invited me to his tent. We had milk and barley pottage and bread, and then slept quite well: saw women grinding in hand-mill. Day hot: bright moon all night.

The manuscript originally began, "On a Wednesday about July 10," but the figures were struck out and replaced by "12," the correct date. This was apparently ascertained from Dr Gracey.

Leben = soured milk, yoghurt.

Khan = caravanserai, oriental inn.

Next day, *Thursday*: Up before sunrise, and out before feeding for Ras el Ain 4 hours: stopped a little before and ate bread and leben in Kurdish tent: chief more hospitable: gave him a hejub to work at Tell Hamra if the English came: money refused. Went on to Ras el Ain ($\frac{1}{2}$ hr.) and stayed there $1\frac{1}{2}$ hrs. drinking and washing: very pleasant spot and good water. In afternoon walked through liquorice and thick dust to Seruj. Took room at Khan and enquired fruitlessly about camera: met Nouri Effendi. Rice and Bahmia with bread. A little feverish.

Hejub = authorisation.

Tell Hamra is an alternative form of Tell Ahmar; the possibilities of excavating this site had just been investigated by a British Museum expedition of which the author was a member.

Liquorice: this wild shrub is protected because its roots yield a substance used in the manufacture of cigarettes as well as in sweets and medicines.

Camera: A camera had been stolen from him at Seruj in September 1909 (*Letters of T. E. Lawrence*, ed. D. Garnett, p. 80).

Bahmia = a vegetable like a small marrow, the French *courgette*.

6

Friday: Up and out for Urfa by carriage (1 med.) after giving ¼ to Khanji: slow drive: saw nothing: Urfa about mid-day (7 hrs.). Took room in great Khan: then went out about 4 P.M. to photograph Castle. Took it from the due West showing the double gates and the line of walls from the πυργοκάστελλος to the extreme end. Warm, beautiful evening, with a little breeze. Rice and bahmia with bread and was then kept awake half the night by a cheap theatre in the café over the street. Police asked for my papers.

Med. = Medjidie, a Turkish coin.
Khanji = innkeeper.
πυργοκάστελλος = the Byzantine equivalent for a Keep or Donjon, the strongest tower of a castle.

7

Saturday: Up late (about 6 A.M.) and went out to the castle. Photographed the castle at the S.E. angle: where the moat turns, and above which is one of the very few Crusader walls in existence here. It is patched in front (to R.) with Arab wall, but is very fine. A wide-angle photo. Then measured the E. side of the moat, and photographed the E. half of the S. side, by wide angle from the bottom of the moat. This makes complete my photographs of the moat, all but the N. side. Then measured this E. half of the S. side, and went and had some bread. Later I called on Gracie and had lunch with him: he mended my Antinous release, and my plummet. After lunch went back to the Castle and measured till 5 P.M. Decided the N. Side moat did not deserve a photo: average depth of moat about 40 feet. Greatest present depth 60 feet, but much filled in. Crusade work is to be found in patches in the entrance gateways, at the S.E. Angle tower, and in a piece of the N. wall. On coming down took a photo of the castle from a

Gracie = Dr Gracey, was then a missionary at Urfa.

little street that runs N.E. This view of the N.E. angle of the castle and the back of the gate-towers looked pretty on account of the amount of green about. In the Khan I found the chief of police and a follower, who remonstrated with me for going about alone. "Boys might throw stones" etc. He insists on a zaptieh to-morrow. Would have slept excellently but for my wisdom tooth. This had me up two or three times. Drank some iced rose-leaf sherbet which quieted it.

This view = Plate V.

Two other photographs survive from a previous visit to Urfa in 1909, one representing the rock-cut moat outside the west entrance, and the other a polygonal tower at a corner of the castle. Both appear in *Crusader Castles*, the latter with a note: "Second visit 1911; climbed this tower and found certain signs of Arab work in it; at the same time the argument may stand, for the foundation is earlier work."

It is hoped to include further information about Urfa in the forthcoming publication of *Crusader Castles*. Meanwhile it need merely be said that the main gateway at the north-east corner has towers extending down the hill; in the photographs from the east the extent of their projection is not clear.

Zaptieh = escort.

ORIENTAL ASSEMBLY

Sunday: Up late (8 A.M.) and had a great wash:
found police waiting for me all round the khan;
went up the castle with one little man. He
complained of the heat, so I sat him under an
arch with some snow and a bowl of water and
tobacco, and he was happy.

Measured the interior etc. A fresh morning
with a cool west breeze. Took a photo of the
interior of the castle from the tall beaked tower
at the W. end: breeze rather troublesome, but
could not get the tripod up: climb rather difficult.
The angle tower is altogether Arabic. Later on
photographed the great gateway (also Arabic)
from the top of a tower. Decided that almost
everything in the place was Arabic except the
moat, some straight pieces of wall, and the S.W.
angle tower: with the two Roman pillars. Offered

Plate VI shows the great gateway on the right.
The two Roman pillars: these columns which, being over
50 feet, figure so prominently on Plates III to VI seem to
have formed part of a temple. A Syriac inscription on one of
them indicates that the dedicator was a local princess. They
stand close to the north wall.

my little man (about 1 P.M. in the khan) a
½-medjidie tip: he took it with thanks, but came
back with it in half an hour, saying he was afraid
the chief of police might hear.   Rested till three,
then walked out to the vineyard and had tea and
supper with the Gracey's: very kind both of
them, but nothing new.   Got back about 9 P.M.

Monday, *July* 17: Up about four, but was a long time getting on the road. The tooth rather worse: an abscess and face painfully one-sided. Bought a metallik of bread, and went over to the castle. Town wall 9–10 feet thick. About 6 started for Harran. No incidents, country everywhere as flat as possible: only huge tells about every two miles: crossed one small stream soon after mid-way. Much mirage: tried to photograph one pool, but failed: nothing showed on the ground-glass. The tower of Harran cathedral was in sight for four hours: all elongated by the mirage, it becked and bobbed in the most fantastic way, now shivering from top to bottom, now bowing to right or left, now a deep curtsey forward. Day very hot: drank five bottles of water between 6 and 2.30: did not stop anywhere on the way. The people rough and unmannerly, half-Turkish spoken, and dressed in rags; children mostly naked. Many camels. Plain all wet, and very fertile. Dhurra, Liquorice, barley, and corn. No springs. Afternoon cloudy: was in

---

Metallik = a copper coin. Tell = mound formed by ancient remains. Dhurra = Indian corn or millet. Tower of Harran Cathedral: The Minaret of the Great Mosque, which is a building of early Christian style.

shade for some moments. Soles of feet very tired. Camera case got very wetted, and back and hinge moulded all out of shape. Fortunately little damp leaked through, apparently. Village people all called me "Sheikh." Stopped outside Harran walls for a short rest, then climbed through a gap into the town. The main part of the village lay to the S.E. of the old site, around the castle. Going there I met a Turkish captain, who spoke French wildly. He was leaving after regulating some recruit business with the Sheikh. I found the Sheikh in the castle, which he has made his house. There was a huge stone vaulted polygonal tower, with deep embrasures and an earth floor. In this he with seven or eight others was reclining, discussing the loss of a key. When I came in he greeted me, and called for rugs and cushions, and then I sat down. He was a young man, perhaps eighteen, with a sharp, rather rapacious and mobile face, and dark curling hair: very broad and tall; of course thin. He had been sheikh only one year, since his father died. We talked a variety of things (they were astonished that I was there so early from Urfa)

He carried the camera slung over his back.

13

and he rather strained my Arabic by asking for a description of English local government, and our marriage customs. He was also curious as to the dignity of sheikh in England. His manners were excellent, very unlike the common people, for he did not snatch at my things, but waited (eagerly) for me to show them him. Some of his men had heard of Jerabis (or Gerabis as they said). They were interested in the coming of the railway. At sundown he brought me food with his own hands: cucumbers, hard-boiled eggs, and excellent wheatbread, while his men dined near us off boiled mulberries and bread. We had some of each. After dinner we talked a little, and then I went out to sleep. He brought me his best quilts, and I slept most perfectly, with his retainers in a heap around me. When I woke in the morning there was an old Turkey cock sitting on a low wall by my head, and many horses in the yard. I was lying on a low platform.

Jerabis = Arabic name for Jerablus or Carchemish, where the author had been excavating and which lay on the projected route of the Baghdad Railway.

Tuesday, July 18: Up by daybreak, and round the outside of the castle. The inside I had explored with the Sheikh the afternoon before. Feet very tired, tooth much worse. Side of face all sore and swollen. The castle built at several periods: part of it quite late; none apparently pre-Arab: mostly of rusticated blocks: there was no ornament anywhere. Huge polygonal towers flank the outer wall, and there is a sort of keep, of smooth stone, with shallow buttress-towers at the corners: inside this is vaulted on two square pillars in one room, others have plain barrel vaults. The castle has had a moat round it: perhaps a wet one. It has been a big strong place, but not over-interesting. The vaulting though is good. Then went and drank coffee (four cups) with the sheikh and his men: about 30 or 40 at the drinking. They spoke un-interestingly. Later walked over to the mosque, and looked for Miss Bell's column-capitals. Took a photo of a lion bas-relief in basalt—5' 2 ins. long, 3' 6" high, 1 foot thick: broken in two

For "the outer wall," of the 9th line, the manuscript reads "the other wall."

Gertrude Bell mentions these column-capitals in her book *The Desert and the Sown.* Lion bas-relief: local work of "Hittite" period (Plate VII).

pieces: rude work. Muzzle broken: lying just outside the East angle of the town wall. A boy behind. Was found on the surface of the ground. Then took a photo of the S. front of the castle, not of the whole of it, but of the eastern half: this showed one small polygonal tower, and a line of walls, with the "donjon" in the centre. Then walked round and took a photo of the great broken tower. Looking into it one could see the floors and the central pier, and the rest of the works of the place. This tower stands on the W. side of the castle, defending one side looking towards the town. The former (S) side looks towards the open desert. Then went across again to the great mosque: could not turn over the other great capital, and found the little ones much damaged underneath: that is, the two I partially cleared. Not very interesting, these little ones.

Then started out seriously to take the Sheikh. Had taken him on horseback with his brother before the S. front of the Castle, and now took him with a friend of his before the tower-room. Also took a photo of his brother etc. Have

The photographs mentioned are Plates VIII, IX, and X.

promised to send him copies of these to Mr. Gracie at Urfa, for distribution: Gracey knows him, and his men come into the town every week.

Then we fed, about 9 A.M., on stewed mulberries, bread, cucumbers, and green-stuff: very satisfactorily: wound up with grapes. Worked at the castle after lunch: measuring etc. Then walked across to Rebekah's well. I came in past it yesterday, resting near it half an hour, and the women as they came out to draw water came and looked at me, singing. Some offered me water from their wooden pails. The well is down steps and very deep, cold, clean water. There are camel troughs near it, possible those that Eleazar used, for such things do not soon wear out. Good water. Drank again to-day. They call it Bir Yakub, and are very proud of it. It is the only well outside the walls. I saw also the Aleppo gate, a poor Arab thing, more ornamental than defensive: in fact the walls of Harran are slight defences: it is certainly not fortified for a siege,

Rebekah's Well (Plate XI), see *Genesis*, chapter 29. Bir Yakub = "Jacob's Well."

Aleppo Gate: illustrated by Preusser, *Nordmesopotamische Baudenkmäler*, pl. 72; other plates show the castle.

Liwan = reception-room.

with its long thin curtains, and shallow towers, all square-angled. The castle is the only fortress. There was a moat, probably wet, all round the town, and between it and the castle. There are no surface signs of pre-Byzantine occupation. The Sheikh is beginning to thaw out: he called me his brother today, which is condescension in a Moslem: but I increased his prestige by holding a sort of levée in his liwan in the morning and answering all questions of all local gentry. The great admiration of my little telephoto tape has led to its disappearance. I went over the castle again, and decided it was all fairly late: post-Saladin at least, possibly post-Crusade. No more photographs needed. The great broken tower is about 60 feet high. It appears from our evening talk that the Sheikh here is only deputy for his elder brother, whom the Government likes in Urfa. They are old régime and Ibrahim Pasha men, with 2500 houses under them. This means a force of 10 to 12 thousand men. A long talk on all subjects in the evening, especially politics: the Sheikh ended by going to sleep with his head on my knee! Ate of bread, grapes and eggs: slept badly with tooth trouble and sand-flies.

Wednesday, July 19: Up about 4, and to the cafe for a time: got the Sheikh to send if possible and find my telephoto tape: very unwilling, for he wanted me to stay over the day, or permanently in the village. Has offered me two first-class wives in his gift. The women here are extremely free, handling one's clothes, and putting their hands in one's pockets quite cheerfully. Also they never pass one without speaking. Messenger came back without the tape: so Sheikh turned out himself, et ne trouva rien dans le village: then he got on a horse, and scoured the country: in about an hour he brought it back. All well! found it with a Turk, who had taken it from my box at Bir Yakub. Then we ate (9 A.M.) of eggs and boiled marrow and bread: after which I took a very ceremonious leave, amid earnest exhortations not to forget the photograph promised. At 10.30 I was off, and went over flat country as far as Simbolat. At all villages I was most warmly entreated to stop: and at one which had a tell, and where I asked for seals the women (who were alone in the village) forced me to enter a house, and rest, asking innumerable questions, and giving me cups of water for drinking and washing. After half an hour I got up to go out, and was given a large handful of bread "since it would be a shame to their houses if one departed empty." These were Arabs. After Simbolat (with Roman ruins) the road disappeared in a rocky hill side, so I had to take again to a compass traverse. By so doing, I reached Silaverik in a couple of hours, and passed it to "Kilar Khass," some Kurd tents in a Roman foundation, where I spend the night. They were hospitable, but the women rude: all Arabic-spoken. I ate wheat boiled in leben, and slept on the new straw of the threshing floor.

Thursday, July 20: Up at four, after a perfect night, thanks to my Kurd host's abba, which kept out the straw most perfectly. Tooth much better: swelling going down: feet sore. Got off about 4.30, and passed over rough hills till 7.30. No water. At 7.30 found a Kurd village which spoke not a word of Arabic. Got bread and leben from them. Half an hour later came down into the plain of Serudj. I had then a very dull five hours plod across the flat, until Serudj was reached about 3 P.M. I bought some bread and cheese, and then slept till about 7, after which I went out and saw Nouri Effendi, and then to sleep. The day had been cool and cloudy, with a shower of rain about 5 P.M.

Abba = cloak.

Friday, July 21: Up about 4.30 after disturbed night: at first very hot, later very cold: no fever. Got off from Serudj about 5 A.M. with a pennyworth of bread. Ate half of it in the first hour's walk: in another hour was in the hills: in the plain was interested these last two days to watch how the wind twists in spirals, often throwing up a thin column of dust many hundreds of feet. This would be done on an otherwise calm day. Walked over the hills for five hours, till I reached the first rivulet of the Euphrates valley: great joy: had a beautiful view from the head of the pass of the Biridjik plain. Stopped at the water for two hours; washed and cleaned up generally: the first clean water I had seen since Sunday. Then about 1 P.M. got going again till 3.30, when stopped at Serudj Kopru. This is a bridge of two arches in limestone, across a green, swift rushing stream: from the sides of the valley just below the bridge come strong cold water-springs. Washed shirt ii and wrote up this account. Biridjik about 1½ hours away. Ate my other halfpennyworth of bread: feet very sore, but

Shirt ii: he was carrying a spare shirt.

otherwise very pleased with the day. Then went on to Biridjik, and saw Basili, and appointed to see the carpenter next day: afterwards met the Khoja, and Yasim and Khalil Jadur in the suk: they very pleased to see me: all came and ate plums in my room in the up-town khan: about 9 P.M. sent them off. A very bad night owing to the multitude of sand-flies. They come perhaps from the trees opposite my windows.

The Khoja or Hoja =Hamoudi, foreman of excavations; see his article in *T. E. Lawrence, by his Friends.*
Suk =bazaar.

Saturday, July 22: Up about 6; repaired feet with bandages (both festering!) and went off to see the carpenter. He says the Tcherkess bought the locks. Arranged with Basili about money if I stay the winter: saw the Kaimmakam and the Commandant about a zaptieh to come from Nizib with me, wrote letters to M. to P.-G., went over the castle, saw the Hoja, and Yasim with our boatman to Tell Hamra: also others from Jerablus. Afterwards bought two halfpenny-worth of bread, and some plums: lay up in the Khan reading and sleeping till 4 P.M. Then went out to the top of the hill, and photographed the town walls etc. from the S. The castle would be behind this hill a little to the L. Then went down into the valley and up hill again. Took the N. half of the castle from the N.E., in the shade against the sun: and the S. half of the castle (both landward side) also from the N.E.,

---

Biridjik Castle (Plate XIII): compare photographs in *Crusader Castles*, fig. 20; Deschamps, *Le Crac des Chevaliers*, pl. vii; Preusser, *Nordmesopotamische Baudenkmäler*, pl. 81.

Tcherkess = Circassian.

Kaimmakam = Governor.

M. = his mother.

P.-G. = Mr H. Pirie-Gordon, the traveller and authority on castles.

a little further on than the one before, and under the same disadvantage of light. This finished my films loaded. The next lot are meant for Rum Kalaat, K. el Nejm, and Aleppo. Tooth rather sore. Thereafter went to bed, first changing films in my room: slept better than last night, but very poorly: all sand-flies again.

Sunday, July 23: Feet better: up about 4, paid for khan and went down to ferry: bought two metalliks of bread, and ate it waiting for the boat: saw Shemali, who said there was now no work in all Jerablus: brought a message from Dahoum, to the effect that the Kala'at was sad.

Then set out from Biredjik for Balkis: road up and down the cliffs: at Belkis nothing at all. Road continued Roman, in one place diving through the rock for a few yards. Road very pretty some hour or two after this: wound up a narrow and deep valley full of wood and fruit trees, to Shard'at a pretty village where I had a row with the Mukdar: he demanded a tezkereh

Dahum, later a great friend of the author's, had been employed by the excavators as donkey-boy. In the letter of June 24 to Mrs Lawrence he is described as "an interesting character: he can read a few words (the only man in the district except the liquorice-king) of Arabic, and altogether has more intelligence than the rank and file. He talks of going into Aleppo to school with the money he has made out of us. I will try and keep an eye on him to see what happens." In 1913, Lawrence brought the Khoja and Dahum to Oxford. The latter died during the War. It is believed that his personality supplied the largest element to the figure of S. A., to whom the *Seven Pillars of Wisdom* is dedicated—"An imaginary person of neutral sex," according to a Note of the Author's.

Kala'at = labourers of the excavations on the Kala'at or mound of Carchemish.

Mukdar, or Mukhdar = mayor.   Tezkereh = permit.

from me: which I refused, he threatened to imprison me, and I turned and twisted him into knots. Ended by his kissing my hand in tears and promising never to be naughty again. Went on another hour, to Kiachtan, where made for house of Mukhdar: was well received, though a little shyly for they are out of the track of travellers. Village is built in steps on the N. side of a narrow valley, running E. into the Euphrates, full of running water, and the wind-noise, rustling up and down the trees. Like Blake's "innumerable dance of leaves." Thought a good deal of his Jerusalem, must have a copy sent out for the winter. Village all Turk-speaking, but an Arabic Tahsildar and a Beyrout zaptieh, with two or three Arabic-speaking people. Ate, about 6.30, of burghul and meat, with stewed apricots and beans, with poor bread. Then about 9 P.M., after coffee they brought me a glorious white and purple quilt, and under that I slept till dawn.

Tahsildar = Collector of Revenue.
Burghul = parched wheat.

Monday, *July* 24: Woke at dawn, to find the village stirring round my roof, which was being swept by a strong cold gale, blowing down the gorge. Set off before 5 for Rum Kala'at. Feet better, tooth better. Road at first led through pistachio groves along the Euphrates bank. Trees like olives, but with leaves like a pear tree. Fruit grows in clusters, shaped like an olive, green at the stub, and growing from yellow to orange at the point. Size of small olives. Road then left river, and climbed a sort of stairway in the cliff, for an hour, to Djarmusly, a cave village in a cleft: then more climb, and almost at once a steep descent to the river banks opposite Khalfata, a village in Mesopotamia, with the house of the Kaimmakam of Rum Kala'at. Went along the river bank (bread and leben from a house) on a sandy path, with fruits and great water, and vines festooned among the trees overhead. This lasted an hour. Reached Rum Kalaat about 10 A.M. The place enormous, a town rather than a fortress. At first came part visible of a huge rock-moat, which cut off the peninsula on the S. (land) side; then the scarp of the Euphrates wall, about 60–90 feet of rock-cutting. I had then to walk up the side-stream valley to the gate of the place, before I could

RUM KALAAT

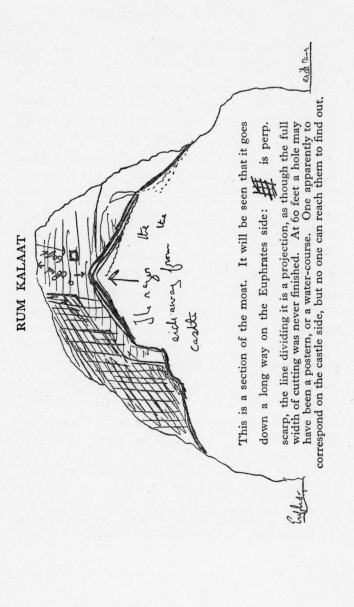

This is a section of the moat. It will be seen that it goes down a long way on the Euphrates side: ⊞ is perp. scarp, the line dividing it is a projection, as though the full width of cutting was never finished. At 60 feet a hole may have been a postern, or a water-course. One apparently to correspond on the castle side, but no one can reach them to find out.

cross it on wide stepping-stones: a broad swift stream, shallow. There was once a bridge. Walked round the far side of the little valley, half-way up. Took a general-view, wide-angle, showing the side stream, the hills and the Euphrates. Another, a little farther on, another (ordinary lens) of the N.E. valley scarp, in shadow mostly. This may be a little fogged. Then went on to the mouth of the valley and took one of the Euphrates front. This has a little domed building like a weli in the foreground. Felt sleepy, so went to cave, and slept till 2 P.M. Got up then, and (i) telephotographed the box-machicoulis of the N.W. angle with a magnification of 13, and a stop of 22°: exposure 12 secs, on normal of 1/50 nom f. 16. This was a large-scale photo of 3 machicoulis. Also (ii) tele-photographed at $3\frac{1}{2}$ mags. L.P. all the range of machicoulis (c. 16) at f. 11 and an exposure of $\frac{1}{2}$ second. Both taken from the shade, and (i) with hood. These machicoulis very remarkable. More about them later. Then went down into

Weli = tomb of holy man.
Photo of 3 machicoulis. Only the right part of this photograph (Plate XIV) is clear enough for reproduction.

castle (down and up!). Through 5 gates, all double and protected by Towers, one monolith, into the outer-court. This in shape of narrow ledge, running N. and S. gate to S. Builders of this place not satisfied with 90 ft. wall and scarp, absolutely perpendicular; but put a rock-moat outside as well: moat once wide and deep; now all stuff of the walls and a graveyard have filled it up. The castle as a whole occupies the narrow point of a peninsula, a rocky ridge, pointing due N. and S. This is surrounded on the E. by the Euphrates, on the W. by the little river Mezman Su, and on the N. by the same: the S. end is thus the only part not precipitous. The crest of the ridge must be between 3 and 400 feet high. This is at the S. end, the highest, but not so high as the rock beyond the castle to N. and S., from both of which it was overlooked, though at a fair distance off. The walls on E. and W. run about half-way up the ridge and from inside them the rocks and ruins pile up, very steeply, to the central pinnacles. The highest point of all is very elaborately carved, and may have been a palace, or a church. The local say a minaret, which is probable, afterwards, but all the orna-ment is not Arab. The building in the N. corner of the ridge-crest is a mosque, with paved court about it. Between this and the "palace" all is destroyed, except substructions and deep cellars cut in the rock. The view is limited, but tremendous. The present village rests across the stream, on the N. bank where it turns E. and W. and extends into the Euphrates. There are poplar trees, and the noise of water. The ridge at the S. end is about 30 feet broad at the top. This is cut down 90 feet to a path about eight feet wide, like the razor in Westmoreland. The moat is about 60 feet wide. I took a photo of it from the Euphrates side, on a point of the castle about 30 feet above the edge of the razor. This is not satisfactory, but gives the river flowing at the bottom very nicely. After this I left the castle (6 P.M.) very tired, but a most glorious place, and crossed the Mezman Su again by the crazy stepping-stones: the hardest I have ever walked over. I went to the little village (Kassaba) to the Mukhdar's. He was away, but a kinsman and his son did the honours of the "house." They were living under a booth of fig-tree poles and oak-branches, and sleeping on top. We ate (about 7 P.M.) of bread, and wheat-leben porridge, and burghul boiled with pepper and pine-kernels. Then to sleep, about 8, fairly successfully, but not like last night which was oblivion. Perhaps

one does sleep better under purple and white silk
coverlets!

From a letter of July 29 to Mrs Lawrence: "The castle of
Rum Kalaat yielded some new points, mostly Arab: it had a
most enormous moat, a perfectly appalling thing. . . . It cut
off a mountain from a mountain, along a col like the coupée at
Sark." It may be helpful to add another traveller's description
of Rum Kalaat; I have summarised it from Nöldeke's article
in *Petermann's Mitteilungen*, 1920. The castle occupies a
promontory of rock, about 400 yards long and 200 yards wide,
which is cut off from its parent hill by an artificial moat about
100 feet deep. Walls cling to the side of the rock, keeping to a
level some 150 feet above the river; while over the centre of the
moat rises a perpendicular scarp at least 100 feet higher.
Entrance to the castle is effected by a path rising on an artificial
ramp overlooked from the west wall (into which at this spot is
built an Armenian inscription, flanked by a pair of stone lions
of the type associated with the Turkish kingdom of the Seljuks).
The path, after passing through a first rock-cut gateway,
mounts steeply on a ledge of rock to the second gateway, which
is of masonry and contains a small side-room. The path
continues on the rocks above the little stream but below the
wall, as far as the third gateway, where it turns and passes
through a doorway in the rock into a small open area outside the
final gateway (which is vaulted). This leads to an Outer
Court, occupying the space between the west wall and the
higher line of rocks on the east. There is also a small gateway
on the east side of the castle, with a staircase cut in the rock,
leading to the bank of the Euphrates. Photographs of the
north and east sides have been published by Nöldeke and in
the *Reisen* of Humann and Puchstein.
The photographs mentioned in the Diary are Plates XVI,
XVII, and XVIII.

Tuesday, July 25: Up at 3.45 (dawn) and had a wash in the stream: ate a cucumber, and had a lesson in bread-making from the women. By the way not a man in the village knows a word of Arabic, so I am rather put to it. All pure Turk, which means very ugly, half-Chinese looking fellows with flat eyes, and broad noses, and wide-split, tight-pulled lips of thin skin. Wrote up this for a time and then stayed to eat, for there is no house but the cave-dwellers between this village and my night-stopping-place. We had burghul and bread together. Then I went along the over-river West-side path, till I could photograph the rock-moat, and returned across the passage perilous, the stepping-stones that I know fairly well by now, to the castle. Feet not very good, tooth again too big for my head. Took a photo of the inside of the monolith tower, showing the applied vaulting. Tower about 17 ft. wide inside between the inner jambs: the third gate counting from outside. The fourth gate, though also monolith, I did not think worth a photo, since it is only a single arch. The fifth is a very fine Arab double-arched gate. All this entrance-masonry is Arab, and very good.

The first two gates have machicoulis over them. Altogether one of the strongest and cleverest

34

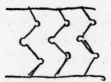

Sketch in the Diary, "Keystones of 5th (innermost) gate
at Rum Kalaat."

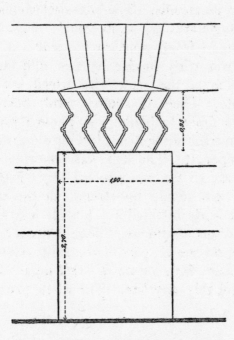

Gateway at Rum Kalaat, after Humann and Puchstein,
Reisen in Kleinasien und Nordsyrien, fig. 26.
(By permission of Deitrich Reimer.)

entrances in existence. The manner in which the roadway is made to double on itself, so that it may be more easily under control, and the right-angled turns at most of the gateways are especially clever. There are no trap machicoulis in the floors, so far as these are preserved, and there were no portscullis. The box-machicoulis of the N.W. angle are very small inside: only one tiny loophole in front, none to the side. A photograph was tried (under lighting difficulties) of the inside of the vault with which they communicate. There is another vault below this, to serve more loopholes. A photograph (w.a.) was also tried of the razor, looking almost directly down upon it. The lens was not wide enough to include all the moat, so the lower part is cut off. There should be enough all the same to make it fairly intelligible. I made a few alterations in my Antinous. Then I looked at the mosque on the N. part of the ridge-crest. It is quite plain, with a date of ١٢٣٦ on a side-door. It is probably very late. The whole place is full

w.a. = wide-angle lens.
The Arabic date = 1236 A.H., which corresponds roughly to A.D. 1858.

of Arab ruins. There is only the foundation of Byzantine stuff anywhere remaining. I left the castle about 9 A.M. by a postern door in a tower on the river side, and walked to Khalfati: I noticed on the way that the people here use gourds, not skins, for swimming the Euphrates: this is here small and narrow, and not as swift as it is later on in its course. Opposite Khalfati wrote up this account. Then climbed up my goat-track most laboriously, and afterwards came down the long shelf of broken rock-stairs, about 500 ft., into the Euphrates plain. Very tiring three hours work. Pushed straight ahead fast through Enesh, Kachtin, and Shardak, to Belkis, a long walk of about 27 miles, with the goat-track thrown in: feet a little sore, but no other damage. Average length of pace after first hour 2′ 7″: afterwards lengthened, till in last hour 2′ 9½″. At Balkis made for house of sheikh, who was hospitable. Fed about 8 P.M. on burghul, shineneh, and bread. Slept extraordinarily well for the E.

On the Euphrates and other Mesopotamian rivers, inflated skins are used, like "water-wings," to give support to swimmers. Shineneh = sour milk.

Wednesday, July 26: Up about 4.30: left an hour later, for Nizib. Road took me up hills at first, and then across a pleasant stream full of springs. After that through olive-yards and vine-yards and fields of liquorice, to Nizib in about an hour and a half. There I bought two half-pennyworth of bread, and the same of grapes, and went to the roof of a khan to eat them. Left about 10 A.M. after drinking an iced sherbet of distilled rose-leaves—a metallik of course—and went down to the bridge over the Nahr Kezin. I drank of this, and then went on to Kefr-Sheikh, the village of Ahmed Effendi, with whom I struck up an acquaintance last time I was out in Syria. I had previously decided not to take with me the zaptieh I had asked for from Biridjik. Feet today nearly right from the blister point of view, and fester on my hand also healed up. This shows there is plenty of reserve force to draw upon yet. On the other hand my right instep has again collapsed. I suppose it will never get over the smash after my leg was broken.

His leg was broken in 1904.

It is painful now in the morning, and after every rest, however short. Ahmed Effendi received me with open arms, and gave me a sweetmeat of burghul and onions and spices, worked into a paste, and leben to wash it down. Not bad, barring the onions, of which I have smelt ever since. Then I looked over a history of Turkey with him (he is educated) and we went together to a spring and garden a few minutes from the house, and talked and drank all the afternoon. It seems he likes arrack! About sunset we came back to the house and sat and talked, he telling beads and smoking. Coffee appeared at times and sustained us till 8.30 when rice and chicken, with iced leben and bread turned up. After this we slept, I very well till sunrise.

Arrack = a spirit distilled from grapes.

Thursday, July 27: Up about 5, and after coffee and a piece of bread on the road by 6. Walked 1½ hrs. to Yarym Tepe, where there is a great spring, dammed up into a pond. Before leaving Kefr Sheikh I bought a little bronze horse found in the fields nearby (¼ med.). Went on to Tell Bashar, where I only stopped to glance at it, bigger than ever as it was, and turned off left at once for Tchiflik, about four hours on the Jerablus road. Country all monotonous. Tried for seals in every village, but found nothing worth getting. Quantities of the more common sort. Prices extremely high in Bashar district. Left foot today altogether right. Right very poor: abscess discharging all day. Bite on right hand begins to fester; left hand healed up—a matter of three weeks. Am now getting gradually into more "Arabic" districts; nearly every one knows a few words here. But since Biredjik I have known more Arabic than any one else I have met: except one boy opposite Khalfati. After 3 P.M. reached Tell Isan on the Aleppo-Biredjik road: very tired. Went on 1½ hrs. and missed my road in striking direct for Yasuf Bey. Finally slept at Nughri, a little place with a "tell" just before Tell Ker. Put up with the Sheikh, who was poor, but hospitable, and had some ideas in his

40

head. He was (e.g.) most forcible in saying that everyone should read: his child is being taught. Fed about 7 P.M. on burghal and bread, with iran. Chaffered about some antikâs and went to sleep.

Iran = a drink composed of yoghurt beaten up with water.
Antika = Arabic for an antique.

Friday, July 28: First of Shâ'ban: next month
Ramadan. Bought my two stones at dawn, for
7½ piastres: found men, unwilling overnight,
waiting for me in the morning. One seal, round,
small, apparently two figures and sacred tree
between. The other an amulet in red stone (seal
in steatite) of the head of an animal: ox, cat, sheep,
horse etc. They came with a small Hittite pot
of "best" Carchemish period (Watergate House)
from the village tell. Left Nughri about 5 A.M.
and walked ¾ of an hour to a village with a stone
of a woman holding her breasts. Proved to be
a miserable Roman sepulchral relief. Went on
to Tell Ker, where ate bread and leben with the
village Effendi: then to Hulman, and so to
Yusuf Beg, Tell Sha'ir, and the great spring in
the valley near Jerablus. This I reached about
12.30. Stayed till 4 P.M., washing, shaving,
repairing, and writing this. Then went on
(1½ hrs.) to Jerablus. Anxious enquiries everywhere if there would be more work, and when the
railway would come. Reached Jerablus about

The British Museum had not yet decided to continue the
excavations for the second season; the Baghdad Railway was
to bridge the Euphrates there and so give much employment.

6 P.M., getting a huge welcome from all parts. The women of the Hoja began to sweep and clean all the place as soon as they saw me over the hills. He himself rushed from the end of the village, and for an hour I held a levée of all the people in the village, and also of Mohammed Jasim, who came in from Kekledji. Their greetings were something to hear. The Haji zaptieh brought me two letters which Thompson had given him in Tell el Hamar. One from mother (June 23) and one from Mr. Hogarth a week later. Apparently a second season not impossible which is the best news I have heard this long time. Very pleasant to have a change of clothes. The Hoja filled me a special waterbottle of water, and gave me great honours and attentions. About 7 P.M. he brought in bread, and fried eggs, and khatir, (yourt) and iran, and then (refusing to eat with me) went out and closed the door after him: this is the highest politeness I have ever met from an Arab. I was most exceedingly comfortable in his house with my big lamp burning and all

Mr R. Campbell Thompson of the British Museum had, with the author as his assistant, excavated for a season at Jerablus and examined Tell Ahmar (Tell el Hamar).

things of mine about me, though I did not, of course, unpack my boxes of stores. About 10 P.M. I went on to the roof and slept, very soundly. Had a headache all the evening, but very pleasant to be with these men again. They are more mannerly than the other arabs. The Hoja very anxious for me to live with him the winter. But the poor man is a most terrible bore conversationally, and sticks to one without end.

Saturday, July 29: Up in time to see the sun rise over the hills of Mesopotamia: very lovely in its colouring as this Carchemish plain always is. Sent off a man to Tell Halesh to the camel-driver to ask why the cement had not come. Found the camel-driver not at home, and no signs of any cement. So just started for the Kalaat to measure the floor of the palace. Hoja started with me, but my distemper of the past two days increased suddenly, so I went on alone. Then it developed unexpectedly in a sharp attack of dysentery. I got on to the Kala'at into a lonely place and lay down on my back, from about 8 till 2.30, feeling most weak and ill. About 3 I sat up and tried to dress, but fainted promptly for about an hour, and again then when I made a second try. Under the circumstances I was afraid to go near the edge of the pit with the measuring tape, and so could not work. About 5 P.M. I got to the village, after a very hard walk. Decided to get out a tin

For Dahum, see the note under date July 23.
Cement: A letter written at Tell Ahmar just before leaving on this journey states an intention of returning to Jerablus "to cement in place the pieces of a large basalt relief that I put together, but which is in the nature of things rather crazy." Kalaat = the mound covering the remains of ancient Carchemish where the excavations had taken place.

of arrowroot, and send a man with letters tonight to bring a carriage from Biredjik. Cannot possibly continue tramp in this condition. Can hardly lift hand to write this. Dreamed when fainting of milk and soda! Sublime. Greeting from every man woman and child in the district I fancy, but I could not see half of them, so only did a poor best at politeness. Fed on arrowroot and milk about 6 P.M. To bed at 8 on the roof: slept well.

Sunday, July 30: Spent the day in the Hoja's house, lying on my back. A good deal of internal trouble. Up about 4.30, fed about 6, on arrow-root and milk. Fainted again about 10 o'clock when a little way from the house, and cut my cheek rather badly on a stone. Rested so, with visitors to see me, till 6 P.M. when I fed, again of arrowroot. Dahum came to see me. Slept about 9.30, badly. Up three four and five times in the seven hours, and had headache besides.

Monday, July 31 : Got up feeling rather wretched, naturally: fed about 8 A.M. No signs of a carriage or of my messenger from Biredjik. Hope he has not bolted with my money. The Hoja awfully good all these days, with me making quite unprecedented demands on his time and patience. But poor man, a most dreadful bore as well, does his best by five or six repeats to get every idea of his into my thick head, which usually understands before he speaks. In the evening tried a little burghul well-boiled in milk. Dahoum came to see me: slept about 9 P.M.

Tuesday, *August* 1: Up at sunrise after a fair night: dawn very glorious, with the broken blacks of the foreground leading to the silver line of the river, crossed by the rough points of the near poplar trees, and then the hills beyond, from deepest black at the water-edge, shaded to grey, purple, and finally a glorious orange, as the light caught them. Sunrise of course poor, as most sunrises are. Ate an egg in milk, and then went down to the river by slow stages, very painfully, and bathed. Needed a wash very badly indeed. River very low, and frothy. Then lay on my back in the house till 4 P.M. when my man came back from Biredjik, without a carriage. The town-doctor would not help him at all, and the Kaimmakam also refused. So now I must delay five days while I wire to Aleppo, or walk to Membidj. Will hope for Membidj: feel better to-day. In the evening again burghul and milk: Dahoum came to see me: slept about 9 P.M.

Wednesday, August 2: Woke up at dawn, which was like yesterday's: slept well on the whole: feel a little better. Ate an egg in milk about 8 A.M. then lay on my back and rested all day. Tcherkess agrees he bought the locks, but says the £3 were a present from Mr. Hogarth! Have written to Selim refusing to pay him anything. The Mukhtar has returned. Yasim wanted to marry, and so wanted money! Mended my things. In the late afternoon walked down to the Kala'at in one spell:—a great feat:—and washed. In the evening chicken-broth and burghul. Dahum came. Slept about 9.30. Felt better all day.

Thursday, August 3: Woke at dawn after a good night feeling very much more alive. Will try for Membidj this evening. Fed about 9 A.M. on chicken-broth and milk. Then opened my two boxes and took out slippers etc. for use on board: have decided to go back to England. Packed also my Rabelais, Holy Grail, Rossetti, and Roland. At midday a little porridge. About 4 P.M. the bottom fell out of the Hoja's hospitality on a sudden. He refused me the loan of his horse, and tacitly refused the Membidj project. Proposed I should rest two or three days in Dahoum's house, and go by water to Tell el Ahmar. There being no boats I could not very well see my way to this, but I struggled down to Jerablus Tahtani, found a horse and hired it, and arranged to start in two hours time for Tell el Ahmar with Dahoum. The boy was necessary for I have no small change with me, and if I cannot change a lira I cannot pay him. Returned at once to Jerablus Fokani and got into thicker clothes and finished my packing. We started about 6 P.M., the Hoja,

Roland = the mediæval *Chanson de Roland.* Lira = Turkish pound.

51

very repentant, seeing me off. About 9 P.M. (marching with a fair moon) reached Sreisat, and slept two hours in the tents of one Mohammed el Kurdi: then started again, moonless, over difficult stony country, losing our way once, for the Euphrates. Reached this before dawn, but found access to the landing-place cut off by the Sadjur, broad, and deep and strong-flowing. Dahoum swam across to bring a boat to help me and the horse over. These two days, Thursday and Friday, thus run together.

Friday, August 4: The sun now rose. Certain people came to see me on the peninsula. They spoke a little Arabic. I feel fairly well this morning, most of the head-dizziness and inclination to faint gone. A boat came after an hour to the shore and I went to the Syrian bank. Then I gave Dahoum a medjidi and sent him off for Jerablus well content. I myself lay down in a hemp plantation till 11.30 sleeping and reading the Holy Graal. At 11.30 a waggon came across, and for want of a better I got on board and went with it very roughly and slowly to Membidj. Here I got eggs and fruit-salad with iced sherbet of lemons, sugared. Tried to arrange a carriage for Aleppo. Had a lot of trouble with various drivers, all asking thrice the fare, but eventually I found a "victoria" going empty to Aleppo, the driver of which was glad to take a lira from me for the trip. It was now evening, and so I ate of a vegetable stew and bread, with iced sherbet of rose leaves for 4d. To bed about 8, in the khan: disturbed night.

Saturday, August 5: Up at three, and on the road a little later. Man has three horses, and so we went well upon the road. Some exceedingly rough stretches all the same. Reached Bab before 9 A.M. Pulled up at the Khan to wait out the midday. Ate a metallik each of bread and grapes. Feel less well than yesterday, but will soon recover this in Aleppo resting. About 2 P.M. went on and reached Aleppo about 7. Drove first to the consulate and recovered a bundle of letters, and then went to Barron's. Fed and then slept most exceeding well.

Barron's Hotel.

Sunday, *August* 6: Up at 5 and read till 7. Then a cup of coffee. Not very well this morning. Wrote letters till dejeuner, and after it: also read a little. About 4 P.M. went out into the bazaar, and saw a little Jew dealer about Hittite seals. In evening fed and slept. Was better after midday, but very shaky all the time. Slept badly owing to excessive heat and the noise: a theatre just outside the house and two street fights with revolvers. Aleppo evidently not decadent in that respect. Police each time 15 minutes late!

Monday, August 7: Up about 4.30, read and wrote letters till 8. Then went out to see about money: raised £10: saw the Consul: settled up with him. Tried after embroidery. In the afternoon saw two antika dealers (one little red seal from one, two black and green from the other): also saw Haj Wahid. Then went with Tagir and looked out Thompson's map of Tell Ahmar: saw Selim: tried the dealers for my lost camera: in the evening read till 8 P.M., when went out to the consul to dinner: much talk after till 12 P.M. Changed films on return to the hotel. Slept well.

Haj Wahid, an Aleppine, had been the expedition's cook at Jerablus.

Tuesday, August 7: Went out with Haj Wahid, and searched the markets from 8 to 12.30 for embroideries: in end found two pieces that may do, for £4 Turkish: did not get more till these pieces approved. All embroideries made big on one size only, 6½ dhras by 1⅓, with a second piece 8 dhras by ¾. The pieces I bought are hand made: they are beginning to machine the stuffs. Then went to consulate and saw Akras: back to hotel to lunch, very tired. In afternoon got out to Ottoman Bank: was ill on return: and lay down all the afternoon dropping off occasionally in semi-faints. Wilkie Young came to see me. In evening felt a little better, and got down to dinner all right: there summed up enough irritation to tell my vis-a-vis he was a pig. Tremendous uproar of Levantines (little man a Greek Jew) 8 or 10 of them shrieking together and dancing about. I was the only person at the table who went on eating. Little man speechless with

Dhra = cubit, of 27 inches or 68 centimetres. The word "embroideries" may be loosely used for woven fabrics, of which the author brought home some pieces made at Aleppo, specimens of which I gave on his instructions to the Victoria and Albert Museum.

astonishment. Sudden irruption from near table of eleven mighty German railway engineers who told little man they had considered throwing him into the river which ran at the bottom of the garden, and would do it at once if he or his friends said another word. An immediate collapse of the Levantine element which ate in whispers and melted silently away after the coffee. Landlord amusing, running round the table during the row wringing his hands and calling aloud in Armenian. Slept exceedingly badly, high fever, great sweating and delirium. Worst night have ever had.

Wednesday, August 8: Got off 5 A.M. for station, 2nd class for Damascus: one only in carriage with me, so slept several hours: saw little en route: ate at Homs in new buffet. Haj Wahid saw me off at the station, and brought a huge water-melon as a present: very delicious on the way. The كانون and I ate it together, and only finished it in the gates of Damascus. Reyak about 5 P.M., Damascus 10 P.M. Went to Palace Hotel. Slept well, though perspired a lot.

The Arabic word *Kanun*, our "canon," means "regulation, law, rule," etc., and its use in the context is obscure. A pun?

Thursday, August 9: Up at 7 A.M. breakfast, and sent for a haircutter: not very good, but quite clean. Afterwards looked over Suifi's stock, but saw nothing worth having. Ditto tiles in the Suk. Got the box with the hauberk I left here in Feb. and started for Beyrout about 1 P.M. Train overcrowded: very uncomfortable and high fever at Ez Zebedani: so went 1st where there was an empty carriage. Slept well there, and felt much better at Reyak where I ate. Continued in empty carriage to Ain Sofar, where irruption of Russian Consul and family: only for $\frac{1}{2}$ an hour; they went out at Aleih. Went on to Beyrout, a little feverish, sleeping much: reached German hotel about 12 P.M. slept very well, though very hot, and perspiring.

Hauberk = a shirt of mail for Mr Charles ffoulkes, the expert on armour (see his article in *T. E. Lawrence by his Friends*).

Friday, *August* 10: Up about 7 A.M. breakfast, and then to Cook to take tickets to England: To Marseilles only finally: Then to P.O. where letter from Will advising come home: to telegraph office to wire so to Mr. Jane: to Sarrafian about films: about 2.30 started by train for Jebail: reached it about 6 P.M.; feeling very well: Miss Holmes in great good-health: saw the new pottery and carried off a few samples: saw my boots: and a wawi's skin. Slept well.

Will = his brother, W. G. Lawrence. Mr Jane = L. C. Jane, the historian. Miss Holmes = Head of American Mission School at Jebail, where the author had spent several long visits. Wawi = Jackal; his young brother had asked for a skin.

Saturday, August 11: Left Miss Holmes about 2 P.M.: got to Beyrout about 5: to hotel straight, and read a few papers etc. till dinner: felt very tired and shaky, but must be getting better since I went up 20 steps at once without resting: to bed about 10 P.M.

Sunday, August 12: Up about 6 A.M. after a very bad night: high fever etc. all the time: Cook came for my things before seven, and managed to get my box of antiques through the customs unopened! This was miraculous after the Jerusalem affair. Tipped him strongly. Boat very full of people: all Syrians apparently.

Left Beyrout about 11 A.M. All over.

ILLUSTRATIONS
TO THE DIARY

Plate I. URFA, "ABRAHAM'S POOL" (which contains sacred fish)
and outbuildings of Mosque

Plate II. URFA, South Side of Castle from the East

Plate III. URFA, East Part of the Exterior of the Castle

Plate IV. URFA, Corner Tower from across Moat

Plate V. URFA, North-East Part of the Exterior of the
Castle with Gate-Towers

Plate VI. Urfa, North-East Part of the Interior of the Castle

Plate VII. Relief of Lion at Harran

Plate VIII.   HARRAN, South Side of the Castle

Plate IX.   HARRAN, Sheikh and Friend

Plate X.   HARRAN, Sheikh's Brother and Others

Plate XI.   HARRAN, "Rebecca's Well"

Plate XII.   VILLAGE OF MUD-HUTS IN HARRAN PLAIN

Plate XIII.   BIRIDJIK, South Half of the Castle from the North-East

Plate XIV.   RUM KALAAT, Machicoulis

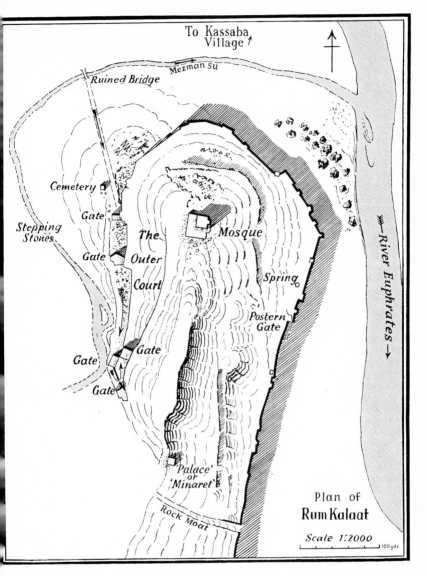

To Kassaba
Village

Mezman Su

Ruined Bridge

Cemetery

Gate

Stepping
Stones

Gate

The
Outer

Court

Mosque

Spring

Gate

Gate

Postern
Gate

Gate

River Euphrates

Palace'
or
'Minaret'

Rock Moat

Plan of
Rum Kalaat

Scale 1:2000

100 yds

Plate XV. Plan of RUM KALAAT

Mostly after Nöldeke (Petermann's *Mitteilungen*, 1920, Plate III)

Plate XVI.   Rum Kalaat, the Moat and "Razor"

Plate XVII.   RUM KALAAT, Double Gateway of Tower

Plate XVIII.   RUM KALAAT, the "Razor" from Above

summed up enough irritation to tell my vis-à-vis he was
a pig. Tremendous uproar of Levantines (little man a Greek again)
8 or 10 of them shrieking together and dancing about. I was
the only person at the table who went on eating. Little man
speechless with astonishment. Sudden irruption from near
table of eleven mighty German railway engineers who
told little man they had considered throwing him into the
river which ran at the bottom of the garden, and would do
it at once, if he or his friends said another word. An
immediate collapse of the Levantine element which ate in
whispers & melted silently away after the coffee. Landlord
amusing, running round the table during the row
wringing his hands and calling aloud in Armenian.
Slept incredibly badly, high fever, great sweating
and delirium. ~~Got off~~ Worst night I have ever had.

Wednesday August 8
Got off 5 A.M. for station, 2nd class for Damascus
one only in carriage with me, so slept several hours:
saw little en route: ate at Homs in new buffet.
Haj Walid saw me off at the station, & brought a
huge water-melon as a present. very delicious on the
way. The قاطب and I ate it together, & only
finished it in the gates of Damascus. Reyak
about 5 P.M. Damascus 10 P.M. Went to
Palace Hotel. Slept well, though perspired a
lot.

Thursday August 9.
Up at 7 A.M. breakfast, and sent for a

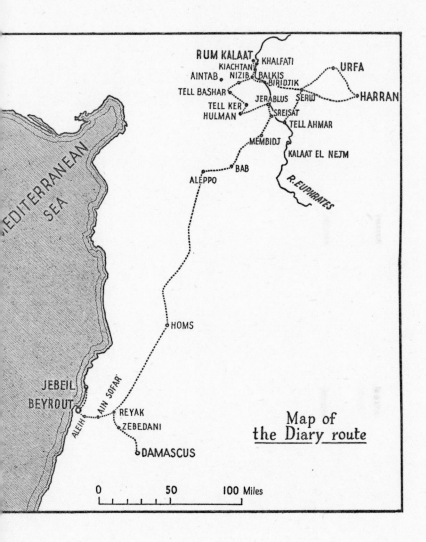

MEDITERRANEAN SEA

RUM KALAAT
KHALFATI
KIACHTAN
AINTAB   NIZIB   BALKIS
BIRIDJIK
TELL BASHAR
JERABLUS   SERIU
TELL KER   SREISAT
HULMAN   TELL AHMAR
MEMBIDJ
KALAAT EL NEJM
BAB
ALEPPO
R. EUPHRATES

URFA
HARRAN

HOMS

JEBEIL
BEYROUT   AIN SOFAR
ALEIH
REYAK
ZEBEDANI
DAMASCUS

Map of
the Diary route

0   50   100 Miles

E

II

THE CHANGING
EAST

EDITOR'S NOTE

THIS article was published in *The Round Table* in September 1920, anonymously, in accordance with the practice of that journal. It is reprinted therefrom by permission of the editor.

A. W. L.

THE CHANGING EAST

A PICTURE-WRITER once coined a phrase, "The Unchanging East," and Time has turned round and taken revenge upon him. The East is to-day the place of change—of changes so great and swift that in comparison with it our Europe is standing still. We have been much engaged lately, making wars and peaces, looking at our own hurts, and trying to restore the balance of the times, and so we have not always been able to spare attention to what Asia is doing or thinking. We have tried to deal with her on the old traditional lines, and to our dismay she has not reacted properly. There have been outbreaks, unrest, protestations, and we, lacking the knowledge of movements there, have missed the sequence and find ourselves reduced to force, as our last remedy and restoration.

Yet there is urgent need for comprehension, of a careful study of our possessions in Asia, in order that we may regain touch with their opinion. We are all agreed as to the need of this stock-taking, though few of us will agree later on the lessons of it. We sent out a commission to India, which considered reform in India; we sent out a commission to Egypt, to consider reform in Egypt. We heard talk the other day in the House of Lords of a commission for Mesopotamia. Even Malta has had one. These all have been piecemeal affairs, conducted by statesmen in blinkers, forbidden to see anything except the political conditions of the province to which they were addressed. None of them gave us a general survey of the new Asia: none of them described the disease as well as the remedy. This disease is physical, material, moral, mental, all you will. It is the civilisation-disease, the inevitable effect of too close contact with the West. The aborigines of Australia got it when they met us, and they died of it. There were biological reasons why their frames were too weak to stand contact with a body social so different from their own. Asia is tougher, older, more numerous, and will not die of us—but indubitably we have made her very ill. Europe is not a thing easily digested.

We see the strain we have put on Asia soonest in the domain of matter. We evolved our own machinery in long centuries of struggle and invention, years in which the face of Europe gradually changed, without any too violent misery, to suit the new ideas: we had pack-horses, solid wheels, springless waggons, coaches, railways, motor cars, aeroplanes: we found the progress indecently fast at times, and put men with red flags to walk before the machines while we breathed—but what of Asia, which has stepped in a lifetime of thirty years from saddle-donkeys to Rolls-Royce cars, from blood-mares to aeroplanes? We grew by slow stages of muskets from bows to automatic guns: it took us five hundred years. The marauder of the desert laid away his spear just before the war, and to-day goes out on his raids with a Maxim. We invented the printing-press four hundred years ago, and served a long apprenticeship by way of wooden types, screw and lever presses, steam presses, electric presses, to the cheap speed of the modern newspaper. The East has side by side the old-fashioned scribe, making each year a poorer living, and the linotype. The vernacular press came to them full-born. These are the material sides. Asia has in thirty years leaped across a stage which took us hundreds. She has not done it very well, perhaps, no better than parts of Russia, parts of the Balkans, parts of South America: the important part is that she has done it, and the Asia of Kinglake and Lamartine is wholly gone. Our eyes show us this, and some of us, the mediævalists, lament it. However, that is just a pose. The clock has never been put back: but the simplest thing in the world is to push its hands a little forward, and there are so many people pushing Asia that it is rather difficult to realise what the unassisted speed of its own ticking is. We will hardly learn this till they stop tinkering at it: yet it is important for us to learn it, since the earth is just a track along which countries and continents race with one another, and for all we know Asia may be gaining on us mentally.

This mental and moral growth is so hard to measure. The material changes prepare our heads to note great change in other ways, but their apprehension stays uncertain. There has been a change in ideas: we hear the people of Asia talking about representative government and parliaments. In our fathers' days they were governed by theocrats and autocrats. We think how long it took England to conceive and bring forth a House of Commons, and we begin to be astonished at this headlong Asia. There are labour troubles in Cairo and Bombay, a general strike in Mecca, trades union congresses in Constantinople. This disease they have caught

quickly.   Self-determination — yes, they have
adopted that: League of Nations—they care
more for it than we do. Things must be moving.
Before the war we saw their politics changing, as
the old springs of action became exhausted, and
new motives came into play. In our fathers' days
the East, and especially the Middle East, this side
of Afghanistan, was logical, similar and simple.
These countries, Persia, Turkey, Egypt and the
rest, were old-established governments, of sultans
and princes ruling by right, often by divine right,
basing their regulations on the dictates of the
state religion. The men were Moslems first, or
Christians, or infidels of some sort. Later on, if
there was any reason for it, they might be Turks
or Arabs, but about this they were not too certain:
the important thing was the faith. We cannot
sneer at them. Only too recently, in the manuscript and crossbow days, we were like them.
About 1870, though, we began to see stirrings of
a new idea, the sense of nationality, which had
been invented in Western Europe, and had moved
slowly south and east, causing turmoil and wars in
the separate countries as it passed. Nationality
is a turbulent principle, and has cost probably as
many lives as religion, in its much briefer reign.
It grew most virulent in its old age: the Balkans

and Ireland, the last places to catch it, have it gravely. We, the older sufferers, seem now nearly immune from it: we may be passing into an economic stage, in which wars and governments will be mainly businesses. It sounds a futile motive of disputes. The economic motive may yet rank with religion and nationality in destructiveness.

However, the Middle East is not as far as this yet. Its first symptoms of nationality were shown in Turkey, when Midhat Pasha began to use French words in government; and in Egypt when Arabi Pasha rose up in arms, and began to drive out the Khedive and his Turkish entourage. Both ideas were sternly discouraged. The English bolstered up the foreign dynasty in Egypt, and Abd el Hamid took up Pan-Islam, a hierarchic conception of Islam, as a corrective to the Midhat notions. He got it from a German book, which had been confusing the Caliphate and the mediæval Papacy. However, the idea had a temporary success, and still holds some ground in India and Africa. For a few years there was peace in Asia, and Europe understood it again without having to change its way of thinking. This was better for Asia and for us, since, as a German pointed out, when we have to change our mind about a thing, we charge our inconvenience also to the account. The new ideas were not dead—indeed, they could not be, with the Balkans offering such a lively breeding ground of nationality-microbes at the gate of Asia: and some twenty or thirty years later they were patent once more, this time not as agitations, but as conspiracies. Persia was full of them: in the end she broke out into disorder and obtained a constitution, whose precise use afterwards puzzled her. She knew that a constitution was the fashionable thing—everybody who was anybody in states had one—but it did not seem to be able to work, itself, and no one in Persia had learnt its habits. However, they still have it, and have had it for ten years.

Turkey then came out strongly, after the British had made some little adjustments in Egypt, as safety-valves for political vapours. Abd el Hamid was stiffer than our Lord Cromer or Sir Eldon Gorst, and so Turkey's nationalism got so pent up that at last it blew him quite off his seat. This was a short end to Pan-Islam: the spiritual and temporal master of Islam was put in prison, and then deposed in favour of a mental degenerate. The old cry would no longer work, as they all in one week took up the new one.

Turkey announced the brotherhood of peoples. The young Turks had forgotten their statistics when they made this statement, but events soon showed them their mistake. The Turks were a minority—perhaps only thirty or thirty-five per cent., in the Ottoman Empire. The subject races, Greeks, Armenians, Albanians, Kurds, Arabs, who formed the rest, could understand the idea of brotherhood, for they had been reading Herbert Spencer and his like for years, and saw at once they they were equal to the Turks, and that it was a sacred duty to go out and help them to establish this new era. So in their millions they began to join together, and think how best to carry on the common government.

Enver and his colleagues struck back in self-defence. They evolved a doctrine of Pan-Turanianism (a doctrine of mixed pedigree, out of a French book and a German book), which taught that the Ottoman Empire must become really Ottoman, and that to its boundaries of 1910 must be added all Turkish-speaking countries in the world. This gave them a broad domestic battle, and a projection later into Khiva and Russian Turkestan. The *irredenta* they decided to leave alone for the moment: first they would make these alien races inside the Empire one. It must be done quickly, for Europe was not looking kindly on them: so they took steps to lop the Greeks and Armenians to the proportions of their bedstead, and began to work upon the Arabs, to teach them Turkish as a first step, and to make them good Ottomans the second. They invented a sharp saying: "A Turkish ass is better than an alien prophet," to teach the people the relative worth of Islam and nationality. The subject races found Enver's little finger very heavy, and began to whisper to one another, in the strictest secrecy, that such things were contrary to the very principles of nationality in whose name they were done. These whisperings increased and became organised, till by 1914 there were healthy conspiracies, aiming to take local autonomy by force from Constantinople, afoot in Armenia, in Kurdistan, in Syria, and in Mesopotamia. Then the war came.

Even before the war we had all Turkey going shipwreck, by her own stupidity. The Turkish race have a fatal habit of obedience, unquestioning obedience, and an equally costly capacity for sacrificing themselves for their state. The first is demonstrated if in a crowded railway station in Turkey you say "Sit down" firmly. At once they all sit down: and the second has been demonstrated times without number during the war in their dogged holding of entrenched positions. Two such qualities imply some innate stupidity in the Turk, and that the native-born possesses in a wonderful degree. He had been a great governor—when government was a crude affair of character and muscle. In these days of telegraphs and high taxation his standard of performance was poor: actually he was not worse than before: only we were better, and so he looked bad. Even at this level he could not find masters of his own: his rulers were Albanians, Bulgars, Circassians, Jews, Armenians, anything but old Turks.

Like his government, so his trade passed away from the Turk. It became scientific, complicated, and he gave it up to the clever races, Jews, Armenians, Arabs, who understood book-keeping and economics. The wealth of Turkey and the manufactures and machinery fell into non-Turk hands. In fact, of his former dominion the Turk kept only the sword—and he tried to change even his sword, which he handled as well or better than any race in Europe, for rifles and big guns and aeroplanes, and in such newfangled things his factor of efficiency soon dropped. He found that they put a premium on brains, and accordingly the meaner races, who used their wits before their hands, gained steadily on him. In the old days a few rusty horsemen had held Tripoli and Albania, and Arabia and Syria, and Mesopotamia and Armenia in subjection. Now each province demanded a substantial garrison. These garrisons had to be real Turks—no others but Anatolians were loyal—and so the conscription every year took a larger and larger percentage of the young generation. These were splendid rank and file, but the old classes were no longer fit for officers. An officer nowadays must read and write, and know a little mathematics, and study Von der Goltz: so they had to find them from the clerkly classes of the towns, sons of officials, and merchants' sons, and westernised young men. They were full of Byzantine vices, and utterly despised the peasant clods who were their soldiers. They neglected all such as did not minister to their pleasure; and with one disease and another, with bad sanitation, bad food, and casualties, the army began to eat up the youth of Turkey. The birth-rate in Anatolia fell, and we who were looking on could see Turkey shrivelling and dying of over-strain. The Italian war, the Balkan wars, were aggravations of an already hopeless state.

Then, when things were in this flux, thus came

the war, and Asia, which had been moving fast for twenty years, put on a dizzy spurt, and left our expectations straining far behind. During the war Europe came bodily to Western Asia. On one side of the fence were the armies of the Germans, on this side the armies of the Allies. Each set great departments, fortified with all their resources, to work on the senses of the Orientals. We talked for and against Holy Wars, as finely as any Moslem dialectician. We preached of the rights of civilisation, of the laws of humanity, of international law, Geneva conventions, Hague conferences. We poured out leaflets, and picture papers, newspapers, films, all to convey an impression which should make the East understand us, and help us with conviction. Like other artists, the character we most illustrated in these productions was our own. The astonished peoples of Western Asia could not choose but hear us, and began, willingly or unwillingly, to see what we were like, and comprehend our least notions. They did not always like them, but they learned a lot. In particular they learned what each of us was fighting for (they heard it from all our mouths, and we all said much the same thing), and a thing sworn to by so many witnesses must surely be true. This liberty, this humanity, this culture, this self-determination, must be very valuable.

In the West, however crude and particular be the war-cry, there will always be an idea or principle behind: though in England you seldom drag the abstract word into the light: it is wiser to let those who think infer it from the illustration, while the vulgar worship the material image. In the East the people are more philosophical by nature, and often care more for the idea than the application. Anyway, they will insist on some abstraction to fill the vacant places of their minds. In the nineteenth century they had had religion, a creed with a body as well as a spirit, one which showed them their road by day as well as by night. They regulated their manners, their meals, their trades, their families, their politics, by its light. The attempt of Abd el Hamid to rationalise this, to make it logical as well as theological, smashed it. When he fell, so did the rule of faith in works. The East remained Moslem, but its public life turned national. People called themselves Egyptians, or Arabs, or Turks, and their newspapers, directed by men emancipated from formal Islam by the influence of western ideas, carried this difference of motive, this new outlook, into the smallest points of life. The abstract standard by which politics and conduct were now judged was this new one of nationality. The nation became the rule of life, the modern creed—and as the war drew on Moslem learnt to go out and fight Moslem, and accept death gladly in battle for the new ideal. When England was at her greatest straits to defend her straggled holdings in the East, these feelings reached their height—and the best measure of their height is not that Indian Moslem fought Turkish Moslem to vindicate the place of India as a partner in our Empire, but that the people of Mecca, the centre of Islam, under its Emir, the Sherif of Mecca, the senior descendant of the Prophet, rose in rebellion against the Caliph, the Sultan of Constantinople, and that this rebellion carried everyone of Arabic speech in Asia at least sympathetically to its side. This was the final triumph, the highest expression there can ever be in Western Asia of the principle of nationality as the foundation of political action, opposed to the principle of a world-religion, a supra-national creed. Not the Galilean but the politician had conquered.

The armistice came, but did not check this movement; it made adherence to it more safe and more rational. The original stalwarts who marched north under Feisal side by side with

Allenby had staked their heads on their fervent belief in an Arab Movement. Their victory made them fashionable, and removed the drawback of campaigning from their programme. Two months after the armistice Syria was nationalist in sentiment from south to north, Egypt was in arms against the British under a like banner, and the young officers of Turkey were banding together against the Sultan (thought to be out of date, silly, and too fond of Europe) to make a new Turkey out of the ruins of the old. They had lost their provinces in Europe—let them go: they had lost their Arabic provinces—let them go. They might lose an Armenian province in the north-east—let it go. They might lose Smyrna— let it go too. Their needs, in this new conception of their national future, were the body of Anatolia, from the Sea of Marmora through Cilicia, to Diarbekir, Erzeroum, Van, Azerbaijan, and even the Caspian. Some day they would cross the Caspian, and attract to their alliance the Turkomans of Turkestan, until all the Turk-speaking peoples to the borders of China were in their orbit. This was the logical Turanianism, the true figure of that which under Enver had been a distorted policy of suppression. Mustafa Kemal, a young, vain, clever, greedy soldier, made himself the leader of the new party, and speedily enrolled under his nominal guidance all the mass of Turks in Asia. His country is self-supporting, and he can sustain without danger the attacks of the Greek Army, and the blockade of the Allies, if he can open friendly relations with Russia on his eastern front. He first tried to approach Italy, and then France, and then England, but found the one insufficient, the other too interested, the third legitimist. He is now blocked from the Ægean by Greek armies, and has to choose between surrender to them and friendship with Russia. The latter will probably mean his own personal downfall, for family reasons: but his followers will not hesitate to sacrifice him, if necessary, for the good of their state. Union with Russia will postpone the dream of an autonomous Turkestan for a generation, and will lock up Turkey in Anatolia proper for so long. Without foreign colonies, foreign wars, and foreign garrisons, she should meanwhile register a large increase of population.

The fate of the Arabs is more difficult to prophesy than that of the Turks, for they are a people of far higher mentality, subtle intellects capable of a depth of thinking, practical intellects capable of a degree of production, inflammable intellects capable of a deal of destruction. They lack system, endurance, organisation. They are incurably slaves of the idea, men of spasms, instable like water, but with something of its penetrating and flood-like character. They have been a government twenty times since the dawn of history, and as often after achievement they have grown tired, and let it fall: but there is no record of any force except success capable of breaking them. The history of their waves of feeling is significant in that the reservoir of all ideas, the birth of all prophecies are shown in the deserts. These empty spaces irresistibly drive their inhabitants to a belief in the oneness and omnipotence of God, by the very contrast of the barrenness of nature, the lack of every distraction and superfluity in life. Arab movements begin in the desert, and usually travel up the shortest way into Syria—for it is remarkable that whereas all prophets go to the desert, yet none of them are ever desert-born. It is the Semitic townsman or villager who receives the revelation. For this reason, for what seemed to be the immemorial finger-sign of history, this present Arab movement, the craving for national independence and self-government, was started in the desert. It, too, took the traditional road to Damascus, the traditional first centre of new movements, and with the successful establishment of Feisal there the second phase was finished. This is not, however, the proper end of the Arab movement: the weight and importance of the Semitic states have always lain in Bagdad, for very sound reasons of economics and population. Syria is a poor country, small and mountainous, dry, lacking in minerals and in arable land. There is no probability that her native population will ever be very dense. Mesopotamia has big rivers, and a huge area of irrigable land. Her wealth in grain and cotton will be very great, and nature may have bestowed on her abundance of cheap fuel. Should that be the case, she will inevitably take the headship of the Arab world in the future, as so often in the past. Damascus may hold an interim pre-eminence: Bagdad must be the ultimate regent, with perhaps five times the population of Syria, and many times its wealth. Mesopotamia will be the master of the Middle East, and the power controlling its destinies will dominate all its neighbours.

The question of a unity of the Arabic peoples in Asia is yet clouded. In the past it has never been a successful experiment, and the least reflection will show that there are large areas, especially of

Arabia, which it would be unprofitable ever to administer. The deserts will probably remain, in the future as in the past, the preserves of inarticulate philosophers. The cultivated districts, Mesopotamia and Syria, have, however, language, race, and interests in common. Till to-day they have always been too vast to form a single country: they are divided, except for a narrow gangway in the north, by an irredeemable waste of flint and gravel: but petrol makes light of deserts, and space is shrinking to-day, when we travel one hundred miles an hour instead of five. The effect of roads, railways, air-ways and telegraph will be to draw these two provinces together, and teach them how like they are: and the needs of Mesopotamian trade will fix attention on the Mediterranean ports. The Arabs are a Mediterranean people, whom no force of circumstances will constrain to the Indian Ocean: further, when Mesopotamia has done her duty by the rivers, there will remain no part for water transport in her life—and the way by rail from Mosul or Bagdad to Alexandretta or Tripoli is more advantageous than the way to Basra. It may well be that Arab unity will come of an overwhelming conviction of the Mesopotamians that their national prosperity demands it.

The future of Persia is also clouded. In the days before the war she was judged for division between Great Britain and Russia. During the war she suffered occasional invasion from Turkey, and was the bed wherein German and British propagandist missions hunted one another. The Russian revolution delivered her from both these pains: England was left the only power capable or inclined to help her out of her bankruptcy and disorder on to the path of decent self-government. Unfortunately the statesmen of the two countries took rather a crude view of the situation, and concluded an agreement open to unfavourable interpretations, not only in the world outside (quite ready to take us at our worst), but in Persia itself. Consequently the advanced elements in Persia deserted us, and began to look across their northern frontier for Russian help. This was forthcoming in minute doses, and they, who included most of the militant spirits in Persia, took active measures against us. Our withdrawal gave them the prestige of a victory, and it seems possible that Persia will either be united under a national and unfriendly administration, or dismembered as before the war, and fought over by Russian and British partisans, nominally Persian subjects.

Egypt, another independent member of the group of new states that the war has sketched in the Middle East, has consolidated herself under pressure of the war and the riots since into the fair semblance of a single people. Her nationalists, who are in reality all the people of Egypt after their degree, have lost their former distinction of Moslem and Christian, and now find a common basis in their geographical situation and their daily speech. They have emancipated themselves from the clerical influence of the Azhar, the old-style Moslem University of Cairo, the former stronghold of pro-Turk or anti-British sentiment. The new nationalists envisage an attack upon this hoary institution, to bring its character and curriculum more into the trend of the present need of Egypt. In questions regarding the position of women and public education they are as advanced as the nationalists of Turkey. Politically their horizon is still very narrow, hardly leaving the banks of the Nile: but there is little doubt that the pressure of surplus population and excess of wealth will soon lead their eyes into larger enterprises, and then the North African question, at present easy to handle in sharply opposed compartments, will become a burning one. Egypt is so much the strongest component of this new North Africa that its government will be able to play in it something of the decisive rôle which the future Mesopotamian government will play in the Arab confederation.

Two new elements of some interest have just set foot in Asia, coming rather as adventurers by sea—the Greeks in Smyrna, and the Jews in Palestine. Of the two efforts the Greek is frankly an armed occupation—a desire to hold a tit-bit of Asiatic Turkey, for reasons of trade and population, and from it to influence affairs in the interior. It appears to have no constructive possibilities so far as the New Asia is concerned. The Jewish experiment is in another class. It is a conscious effort, on the part of the least European people in Europe, to make head against the drift of the ages, and return once more to the Orient from which they came. The colonists will take back with them to the land which they occupied for some centuries before the Christian era samples of all the knowledge and technique of Europe. They propose to settle down amongst the existing Arabic-speaking population of the country, a people of kindred origin, but far different social condition. They hope to adjust their mode of life to the climate of Palestine, and by the exercise of their skill and capital to make it as highly

organised as a European state. The success of
their scheme will involve inevitably the raising of
the present Arab population to their own material
level, only a little after themselves in point of time,
and the consequences might be of the highest
importance for the future of the Arab world. It
might well prove a source of technical supply
rendering them independent of industrial Europe,
and in that case the new confederation might
become a formidable element of world power.
However, such a contingency will not be for the
first or even for the second generation, but it
must be borne in mind in any laying out of
foundations of empire in Western Asia. These
to a very large extent must stand or fall by the
course of the Zionist effort, and by the course of
events in Russia.

It is curious how with each modification of the
condition of Russia her potential influence has
steadily increased in South-Western Asia. Since
the Czarist days Russia has been sole arbiter of
Northern Asia, from the Black Sea to the China
Sea, and so large a proportion of her bulk lies in
Asia that there is real reason for considering her
revolution an Asiatic phenomenon. It has at
least a very strong Asiatic importance, and may
well yet do for Asia what the kindred revolution

in France did for Europe, after a parallel cycle of some sixty years. It is not that the doctrines of Lenin find a ready echo in the minds of the peasantry of Asia—they have not found their warmest adherents in the peasantry of Russia: but the Bolshevist success has been a potent example to the East of the overthrow of an ancient government, depending on a kind of divine right, and weighing on Asia with all the force of an immense military establishment. Its fall has not affected the division of Asia, north to Russia and south to England: it has changed the Russian area from an area of effective domination to an area of influence, a base of preaching or action for the advanced members of every society. Further, it will provide a frontier permanently open, and an unlimited source of armament. In the old days the Russian Imperial Government kept their southern frontier along the hillcrests of central Asia strictly to themselves, and thus there was little coming or going between our half and theirs. This is now changed, and the progressive part of Asia has become the North and not the South. Upon the action, not of the Russian Government, but of private individuals sharing the anti-imperialist views of the Russian State, and willing to work as private individuals

94

to spread their beliefs in Southern Asia, depends much of the future of Persia, of Anatolia, and to a lesser degree of Syria and Mesopotamia. The two temporary republics of Armenia and Georgia may be said to be Russian in a more direct fashion.

This new condition, of a conscious and logical political nationalism, now the dominant factor of every indigenous movement in Western Asia, is too universal to be extinguished, too widespread to be temporary. We must prepare ourselves for its continuance, and for a continuance of the unrest produced by it in every contested district, until such time as it has succeeded and passed into a more advanced phase. It is so radical a change in the former complexion of Western Asia as to demand from us a revision of the principles of our policy in the Middle East, and an effort to adjust ourselves, that the advantage of its constructive elements may be on our side.

This new Imperialism is not just withdrawal and neglect on our part. It involves an active side of imposing responsibility on the local peoples. It is what they clamour for, but an unpopular gift when given. We have to demand from them provision for their own defence. This is the first stage towards self-respect in peoples. They must find their own troops to replace our armies of occupation which we are going to withdraw. For this they must be armed, and must learn by having arms not to misuse them. We can only teach them how by forcing them to try, while we stand by and give advice. This is not for us less honourable than administration: indeed, it is more exacting, for it is simple to give orders, but difficult to persuade another to take advice, and it is the more difficult which is most pleasant doing. We have to be prepared to see them doing things by methods quite unlike our own, and less well: but on principle it is better that they half-do it than that we do it perfectly for them. In pursuing such courses we will find our best helpers not in our former most obedient subjects, but among those now most active in agitating against us, for it will be the intellectual leaders of the people who will serve the purpose, and these are not the philosophers nor the rich, but the demagogues and the politicians. It seems a curious class to which to entrust the carefully begun edifices of our colonial governments—but in essence it will not be dissimilar to the members of our own House of Commons, whom we entrust with our own liberties. They will not wish to take charge, but we can force their hand by preparing to go. We do not risk losing them to another power—for the Englishman is liked by everyone who has not too much to do with him, and the British Empire is so much the largest concern in the world that it offers un-rivalled inducements to small peoples to join it. Egypt, Persia and Mesopotamia, if assured of eventual dominion status, and present internal autonomy, would be delighted to affiliate with us, and would then cost us no more in men and money than Canada or Australia. The alternative is to hold on to them with ever-lessening force, till the anarchy is too expensive, and we let go.

III

THE EVOLUTION
OF A REVOLT

EDITOR'S NOTE

THIS article formed part of the first number of *The Army Quarterly*, in October 1920, and is here reprinted therefrom by permission of the editor and of the publishers, Messrs Wm. Clowes & Sons. Some of the contents were subsequently utilised in Chapter xxxiii of *Seven Pillars of Wisdom*.

A. W. L.

THE EVOLUTION OF A REVOLT

THE Arab Revolt began in June, 1916, with an Arab offensive, a surprise attack by the half-armed and inexperienced tribesmen upon the Turkish garrisons in Medina and about Mecca. They had no success, and after a few days' effort they withdrew out of range of the fort artillery, and began a blockade. This method forced the early surrender of Mecca, whose road communications were too long and rough to be held by the Turks. Medina, however, was linked by railway to the Turkish main Army in Syria, and, thanks to their superior numbers and equipment, the Turks were able in a week's fighting to restore the line and reinforce the temporarily-besieged garrison there. The Arab forces which had attacked it fell back gradually as the Turks became more offensive, and at last moved fifty miles south-west into the hills, and there took up a position across the main road to Mecca.

At this point the campaign stood still for many weeks, while both sides breathed, and the Turks prepared to take the initiative, by sending an expeditionary force to Mecca, to crush the revolt where it had started. They moved an army corps to Medina by rail, and strengthened it beyond establishment with guns, cars, aeroplanes, machine guns, and quantities of horse, mule and camel transport. Then they began to advance down the main western road from Medina to Mecca. The total distance was about two hundred and fifty miles. The first fifty miles were easy: then came a belt of hills twenty miles wide, in which were Feisal's tribesmen standing on the defensive: after the hills was a level stretch, for seventy miles along the coastal plain to Rabegh, rather more than half-way. Rabegh is a little port on the Red Sea, with good anchorage for ships. In it was Sherif Ali, Feisal's eldest brother, with more tribal forces, and the beginnings of an Arab Regular Army, recruited from officers and men of Arab blood, who had served in the Turkish Army, and were now willing to fight against their old masters for their national freedom.

Our military advisers had told us that Rabegh was the key of Mecca, since no hostile force could pass along the main road without occupying it and watering at its wells under the palm trees. Its defence was therefore of the main importance. The Navy could co-operate effectively from the harbour, and the circle of the palm-groves must be laid out as an entrenched position, and held by regular troops. They thought that Beduin tribesmen would never be of any value in a fixed position, and that therefore an Arab regular force must be formed and trained as soon as possible to undertake this duty. If the Turks advanced before the new force was ready, the British would have to lend a brigade, of British or Allied troops, to save the Sherif in his extremity, by maintaining this stop-block.

A personal reconnaissance of the Arab positions, here and in the hills where Feisal was, caused me to modify the views of the experts slightly. Feisal had some thousands of men, all armed with rifles, rather casual, distrustful fellows, but very active and cheerful. They were posted in hills and defiles of such natural strength that it seemed to me very improbable that the Turks could force them, just by their superior numbers: for in some ways it is easier to defend a range of hills against nine or ten thousand men than against nine or ten. Accordingly, I reported that the tribesmen (if strengthened by light machine guns, and regular officers as advisers) should be able to hold up the Turks indefinitely, while the Arab regular force was being created. As was almost inevitable in view of the general course of military thinking since Napoleon, we all looked only to the regulars to win the war. We were obsessed by the dictum of Foch that the ethic of modern war is to seek for the enemy's army, his centre of power, and destroy it in battle. Irregulars would not attack positions and so they seemed to us incapable of forcing a decision.

While we were training the regulars (of course not sending officers or light machine guns to Feisal in the hills meanwhile), the Turks suddenly put my appreciation to the test by beginning their advance on Mecca. They broke through my "impregnable" hills in twenty-four hours, and came forward from them towards Rabegh slowly. So they proved to us the second theorem of irregular war—namely, that irregular troops are as unable to defend a point or line as they are to attack it.

This lesson was received by us quite without gratitude, for the Turkish success put us in a critical position. The Rabegh force was not capable of repelling the attack of a single battalion, much less of a corps. It was nearly impossible to send down British troops from Egypt at the moment: nor do I think that a single British brigade would have been capable of holding all the Rabegh position: nor was the Rabegh position indispensable to the Turks: nor would a single Arab have remained with the Sherif if he introduced British troops into the Hejaz.

In the emergency it occurred to me that perhaps the virtue of irregulars lay in depth, not in face, and that it had been the threat of attack by them upon the Turkish northern flank which had made the enemy hesitate for so long. The actual Turkish flank ran from their front line to Medina, a distance of some fifty miles: but, if we moved towards the Hejaz railway behind Medina, we might stretch our threat (and, accordingly, their flank) as far, potentially, as Damascus, eight hundred miles away to the north. Such a move would force the Turks to the defensive, and we might regain the initiative. Anyhow, it seemed our only chance, and so, in January, 1917, we took all Feisal's tribesmen, turned our backs on Mecca, Rabegh and the Turks, and marched away north two hundred miles to Wejh, thanks to the help of the British Red Sea Fleet, which fed and watered us along the coast, and gave us gun-power and a landing party at our objective.

This eccentric movement acted like a charm. Clausewitz had said that rearguards modulate the enemy's action like a pendulum, not by what they do, but by their mere existence. We did nothing concrete, but our march recalled the Turks (who were almost into Rabegh) all the way back to Medina, and there they halved their force. One half took up the entrenched position about the city, which they held until after the Armistice. The other half was distributed along the railway to defend it against our threat. For the rest of the war the Turks stood on the defensive against us, and we won advantage over advantage till, when peace came, we had taken thirty-five thousand prisoners, killed and wounded and worn out about as many, and occupied a hundred thousand square miles of the enemy's territory, at little loss to ourselves.

However, we were not then aware that Wejh was our turning-point. We thought we had come to it to cut the railway, and I was at once sent up country to do this, as a means to take Medina, the Turkish headquarters and main garrison. On the way up I fell ill, and spent ten days on my back in a tent, without anything to do except to think about war and analyse our hitherto empirical practice for its real import.

I was unfortunately as much in charge of the campaign as I pleased, and had had no training in command to fit me for such a work. In military theory I was tolerably read, for curiosity in Oxford years before had taken me past Napoleon to Clausewitz and his school, to Caemmerer and Moltke, Goltz and the recent Frenchmen. These had seemed very partial books, and after a look at Jomini and Willisen I had found broader principles in the eighteenth century, in Saxe, Guibert and their followers. However, Clausewitz was intellectually so much the master of them all that unwillingly I had come to believe in him. Tactically the only campaigns I had studied step by step were the ancient affairs of Hannibal and Belisarius, Mohammed and the Crusades! My interests were only in pure theory and I looked everywhere for the metaphysical side, the philosophy of war, about which I thought a little for some years. Now I was compelled suddenly to action, to find an immediate equation between my book-reading and our present movements.

However, the books gave me the aim in war quite pat, "the destruction of the organised forces of the enemy" by "the one process battle." Victory could only be purchased by blood. This was a hard saying for us, as the Arabs had no organised forces, and so a Turkish Foch would have no aim: and the Arabs would not endure casualties, so that an Arab Clausewitz could not buy his victory. These wise men must be talking metaphors, for we were indubitably winning our war . . . and as I thought about it, it dawned on me that we had won the Hejaz war. We were in occupation of 99 per cent. of the Hejaz. The Turks were welcome to the other fraction till peace or doomsday showed them the futility of clinging to our window pane. This part of the war was over, so why bother about Medina? It was no base for us, like Rabegh, no threat to the Turks, like Wejh: just a blind alley for both. The Turks sat in it on the defensive, immobile, eating for food the transport animals which were to have moved them to Mecca, but for which there was no pasture in their now restricted lines. They were harmless sitting there; if we took them prisoner, they would cost us food and guards in Egypt: if we drove them out northward into Syria, they would join the main Army blocking us in Sinai. On all counts they were best where they were, and they valued Medina and wanted to keep it. Let them!

This seemed unlike the ritual of war of which Foch had been priest, and so I began to hope that there was a difference of kind between us and him. He called his modern war "absolute." In it two nations professing incompatible philosophies set out to try them in the light of force. A struggle of two immaterial principles could only end when the supporters of one had no more means of resistance. An opinion can be argued with: a conviction is best shot. The logical end of a war of creeds is the final destruction of one, and Salammbo the classical textbook-instance. These were the lines of the struggle between France and Germany, but not, I thought, between Germany and England, for all efforts to make our men hate the enemy just made them hate war, and later on by the Armistice we made the Great War fall short of the Foch ideal. To me it seemed only a variety of war: and I could then see other sorts, as Clausewitz had numbered them, personal wars for dynastic reasons, expulsive wars for party reasons, commercial wars for trading reasons.

Then I thought of the Arab aim, and saw that it was geographical, to occupy all Arabic-speaking lands in Asia. In the doing of it we might kill Turks: we disliked them very much. Yet "killing Turks" would never be an excuse or aim. If they would go quietly, our war would end. If not, we would try to drive them out: in the last resort we would be compelled to the desperate course of blood, on the maxim of "murder" war, but as cheaply as possible for ourselves, since the Arabs were fighting for freedom, a pleasure only to be tasted by a man alive.

My own personal duty was command, and I began to unravel command and analyse it, both from the point of view of strategy, the aim in war, the synoptic regard which sees everything by the standard of the whole, and from the point of view called tactics, the means towards the strategic end, the steps of its staircase. In each I found the same elements, one algebraical, one biological, a third psychological. The first seemed a pure science, subject to the laws of mathematics, without humanity. It dealt with known invariables, fixed conditions, space and time, inorganic things like hills and climates and railways, with mankind in type-masses too great for individual variety, with all artificial aids, and the extensions given our faculties by mechanical invention. It was essentially formulable.

In the Arab case the algebraic factor would take first account of the area we wished to conquer, and I began idly to calculate how many square miles . . . perhaps a hundred and forty thousand . . . and how would the Turks defend all that . . . no doubt by a trench line across the bottom, if we were an army attacking with banners displayed . . . but suppose we were an influence (as we might be), an idea, a thing invulnerable, intangible, without front or back, drifting about like a gas? Armies were like plants, immobile as a whole, firm-rooted, nourished through long stems to the head. We might be a vapour, blowing where we listed. Our kingdoms lay in each man's mind, and as we wanted nothing material to live on, so perhaps we offered nothing material to the killing. It seemed a regular soldier might be helpless without a target. He would own the ground he sat on, and what he could poke his rifle at.

Then I estimated how many posts they would need to contain this attack in depth, sedition putting up her head in every unoccupied one of these hundred thousand square miles. I knew the Turkish Army inside and out, and allowing for its recent extension of faculty by guns and aeroplanes and armoured trains, still it seemed it would have need of a fortified post every four square miles, and a post could not be less than twenty men. The Turks would need six hundred thousand men to meet the combined ill wills of all the local Arab people. They had one hundred thousand men available. It seemed the assets in this part of command were ours, and climate, railways, deserts, technical weapons could also be attached to our interests, if we realised our raw materials and were apt with them. The Turk was stupid and would believe that rebellion was absolute, like war, and deal with it on the analogy of absolute warfare. Analogy is fudge, anyhow, and to make war upon rebellion is messy and slow, like eating soup with a knife.

So much for the mathematical element, which I annoyed the others by calling hecastics. The second factor was biological, the breaking-point, life and death, or better, wear and tear. Bionomics seemed a good name for it. The war-philosophers had properly made it an art, and had elevated one item in it, "effusion of blood," to the height of a principle. It became humanity in battle, an art touching every side of our corporal being, and very warm. There was a line of variability (man) running through all its estimates. Its components were sensitive and illogical, and generals guarded themselves by the device of a reserve, the significant medium of their art. Goltz had said that when you know the enemy's strength, and he is fully deployed, then you know enough to dispense with a reserve. But this is never. There is always the possibility of accident, of some flaw in materials, present in the general's mind: and the reserve is unconsciously held to meet it. There is a "felt" element in troops, not expressible in figures, guessed at by the equivalent of δόξα in Plato, and the greatest commander is he whose intuitions most nearly happen. Nine-tenths of tactics are certain, and taught in books: but the irrational tenth is like the kingfisher flashing across the pool, and that is the test of generals. It can only be ensued by instinct sharpened by thought practising the stroke so often that at the crisis it is as natural as a reflex.

Yet to limit the art to humanity seemed to me an undue narrowing down. It must apply to materials as much as to organisms. In the Turkish Army materials were scarce and precious, men more plentiful than equipment. Conse-quently our cue should be to destroy not the Army but the materials. The death of a Turkish bridge or rail, machine or gun, or high explosive was more profitable to us than the death of a Turk. The Arab Army just now was equally chary of men and materials: of men because they being irregulars were not units, but individuals, and an individual casualty is like a pebble dropped in water: each may make only a brief hole, but rings of sorrow widen out from them. We could not afford casualties. Materials were easier to deal with and put straight. It was our obvious duty to make ourselves superior in some one branch, gun-cotton or machine guns, or whatever could be made most decisive. Foch had laid down the maxim, applying it to men, of being superior at the critical point and moment of attack. We might apply it to materials, and be superior in equipment in one dominant moment or respect.

For both men and things we might try to give Foch's doctrine a negative twisted side, for cheapness' sake, and be weaker than the enemy everywhere except in one point or matter. Most wars are wars of contact, both forces striving to keep in touch to avoid tactical surprise. Our war should be a war of detachment: we were to contain the enemy by the silent threat of a vast unknown desert, not disclosing ourselves till the moment of attack. This attack need be only nominal, directed not against his men, but against his materials: so it should not seek for his main strength or his weaknesses, but for his most accessible material. In railway cutting this would be usually an empty stretch of rail. That was a tactical success. We might turn the average into a rule (not a law—war is antinomian, said Colin), and at length we developed an unconscious habit of never engaging the enemy at all. This chimed with the numerical plea of never giving the enemy's soldier a target. Many Turks on our front had no chance all the war to fire a shot at us, and correspondingly we were never on the defensive, except by rare accident. The corollary of such a rule was perfect "intelligence," so that we could plan in complete certainty. The chief agent had to be the general's head (de Feuquière said this first), and his knowledge had to be faultless, leaving no room for chance. We took more pains in this service than any other staff I saw.

The third factor in command seemed to be the psychological, that science (Xenophon called it diathetic) of which our propaganda is a stained and ignoble part. Some of it concerns the crowd, the adjustment of spirit to the point where it becomes fit to exploit in action, the prearrangement of a changing opinion to a certain end. Some of it deals with individuals, and then it becomes a rare art of human kindness, transcending, by purposeful emotion, the gradual logical sequence of our minds. It considers the capacity for mood of our men, their complexities and mutability, and the cultivation of what in them profits the intention. We had to arrange their minds in order of battle, just as carefully and as formally as other officers arranged their bodies: and not only our own men's minds, though them first: the minds of the enemy, so far as we could reach them: and thirdly, the mind of the nation supporting us behind the firing-line, and the mind of the hostile nation waiting the verdict, and the neutrals looking on.

It was the ethical in war, and the process on which we mainly depended for victory on the Arab front. The printing press is the greatest weapon in the armoury of the modern commander, and we, being amateurs in the art of command, began our war in the atmosphere of the twentieth century, and thought of our weapons without prejudice, not distinguishing one from another socially. The regular officer has the tradition of forty generations of serving soldiers behind him, and to him the old weapons are the most honoured. We had seldom to concern ourselves with what our men did, but much with what they thought, and to us the diathetic was more than half command. In Europe it was set a little aside and entrusted to men outside the General Staff. In Asia we were so weak physically that we could not let the metaphysical weapon rust unused. We had won a province when we had taught the civilians in it to die for our ideal of freedom: the presence or absence of the enemy was a secondary matter.

These reasonings showed me that the idea of assaulting Medina, or even of starving it quickly into surrender was not in accord with our best strategy. We wanted the enemy to stay in Medina, and in every other harmless place, in the largest numbers. The factor of food would eventually confine him to the railways, but he was welcome to the Hejaz railway, and the Trans-Jordan railway, and the Palestine and Damascus and Aleppo railways for the duration of the war, so long as he gave us the other nine hundred and ninety-nine thousandths of the Arab world. If he showed a disposition to evacuate too soon, as a step to concentrating in the small area which his numbers could dominate effectively, then we would have to try and restore his confidence, not harshly, but by reducing our enterprises against him. Our ideal was to keep his railway just working, but only just, with the maximum of loss and discomfort to him.

Accordingly, I put in a few damages to the line, enough to annoy the enemy without making him fear its final destruction, and then rode back to Wejh, to explain to my chiefs that the Arab war was geographical, and the Turkish Army for us an accident, not a target. Our aim was to seek its weakest link, and bear only on that till time made the mass of it fall. Our largest available resources were the tribesmen, men quite unused to formal warfare, whose assets were movement, endurance, individual intelligence, knowledge of the country, courage. We must impose the longest possible passive defence on the Turks (this being the most materially expensive form of war) by extending our own front to its maximum. Tactically we must develop a highly mobile, highly equipped type of army, of the smallest size, and use it successively at distributed points of the Turkish line, to make the Turks reinforce their occupying posts beyond the economic minimum of twenty men. The power of this striking force of ours would not be reckoned merely by its strength. The ratio between number and area determined the character of the war, and by having five times the mobility of the Turks we could be on terms with them with one-fifth their number.

Our success was certain, to be proved by paper and pencil as soon as the proportion of space and number had been learned. The contest was not physical, but mineral, and so battles were a mistake. All we won in a battle was the ammunition the enemy fired off. Our victory lay not in battles, but in occupying square miles of country. Napoleon had said it was rare to find generals willing to fight battles. The curse of this war was that so few could do anything else. Napoleon had spoken in angry reaction against the excessive finesse of the eighteenth century, when men almost forgot that war gave licence to murder. We had been swinging out on his dictum for a hundred years, and it was time to go back a bit again. Battles are impositions on the side which believes itself weaker, made unavoidable either by lack of land-room, or by the need to defend a material property dearer than the lives of soldiers. We had nothing material to lose, so we were to defend nothing and to shoot nothing. The precious element of our forces were the Beduin irregulars, and not the regulars whose rôle would only be to occupy places to which the irregulars had already given access. Our cards were speed and time, not hitting power, and these gave us strategical rather than tactical strength. Range is more to strategy than force. The invention of bully-beef has modified land-war more profoundly than the invention of gunpowder.

My chiefs did not follow all these arguments, but gave me leave to try my hand after my own fashion. We went off first to Akaba, and took it easily. Then we took Tafileh and the Dead Sea: then Azrak and Deraa, and finally Damascus, all in successive stages worked out consciously on these sick-bed theories. The process was to set up ladders of tribes, giving us a safe and comfortable route from our sea-bases (Yenbo, Wejh or Akaba) to our advanced bases of operation. These were sometimes three hundred miles away, a long distance in lands without railways or roads, but made short for us by an assiduous cultivation of desert-power, control by camel parties of the desolate and unmapped wilderness which fills up all the centre of Arabia, from Mecca to Aleppo and Bagdad.

In character these operations were more like naval warfare than ordinary land operations, in their mobility, their ubiquity, their independence of bases and communications, their lack of ground features, of strategic areas, of fixed directions, of fixed points. "He who commands the sea is at great liberty, and may take as much or as little of the war as he will": he who commands the desert is equally fortunate. Camel raiding-parties, as self-contained as ships, could cruise without danger along any part of the enemy's land-frontier, just out of sight of his posts along the edge of cultivation, and tap or raid into his lines where it seemed fittest or easiest or most profitable, with a sure retreat always behind them into an element which the Turks could not enter. We were fortified in our freedom of movement by an intimate knowledge of the desert-front of Syria, a country peculiarly and historically indefensible against attack from the east. I had traversed most of it on foot before the war many times, working out the movements of Saladin or Ibrahim Pasha, and, as our war-experience deepened, we became adepts at that form of geographical intuition, described by Bourcet as wedding unknown land to known in a mental map.

Our tactics were always tip and run, not pushes, but strokes. We never tried to maintain or improve an advantage, but to move off and strike again somewhere else. We used the smallest force, in the quickest time, at the farthest place. If the action had continued till the enemy had changed his dispositions to resist it, we would have been breaking the spirit of our fundamental rule of denying him targets.

The necessary speed and range were attained by the extreme frugality of the desert men, and their high efficiency when mounted on their she-riding-camels. The camel is an intricate animal, and calls for skilled labour in the handling: but she yields a remarkable return. We had no system of supply: each man was self-contained and carried on the saddle, from the sea base at which the raid started, six weeks' food for himself. The six-weeks' ration for ordinary men was a half-bag of flour, forty-five pounds in weight. Luxurious feeders carried some rice also for variety. Each man baked for himself, kneading his own flour into unleavened cakes, and warming it in the ashes of a fire. We carried about a pint of drinking water each, since the camels required to come to water on average every three days, and there was no advantage in our being richer than our mounts. Some of us never drank between wells, but those were hardy men: most of us drank a lot at each well, and had a drink during the intermediate dry day. In the heat of summer Arabian camels will do about two hundred and fifty miles comfortably between drinks: and this represented three days' vigorous marching. The country is not so dry as it is painted, and this radius was always more than we needed. Wells are seldom more than one hundred miles apart. An easy day's march was fifty miles: an emergency march might be up to one hundred and ten miles in the day.

THE EVOLUTION OF A REVOLT

The six weeks' food gave us a range of over a thousand miles out and home, and that (like the pint of water) was more than ever we needed, even in so large a country as Arabia. It was possible (for me, the camel-novice in the Army, "painful" was a better word) to ride fifteen hundred miles in the month without re-victualling, and there was never a fear of starvation, for each of us was riding on two hundred pounds of potential meat, and when food lacked we would stop and eat the weakest of our camels. Exhausted camel is poor food, but cheaper killing than a fat one, and we had to remember that our future efficiency depended on the number of good camels at our disposal. They lived on grazing as we marched (we never gave them grain or fodder), and after their six weeks on the road they would be worn thin, and have to be sent to pasture for some months' rest, while we called out another tribe in replacement, or found fresh riding-beasts.

We did not hamper ourselves with led-camels. The men carried with them a hundred rounds of ammunition and a rifle, or else two men would be an "automatic" team, dividing the gun and its drums between them. They slept as they were, in their riding cloaks, and fared well enough till the winter of 1917–1918, which caught us on the five-thousand foothills of Edom behind the Dead Sea. Then we lost many men and camels frozen to death, or trapped in the snow, which lay over all the high lands in deep drifts for weeks, while we vainly appealed to Egypt for tents and boots and blankets. In reply we were advised that Arabia was a tropical country!

The equipment of the raiding parties aimed at simplicity, with nevertheless a technical superiority over the Turks in the most critical department. We had great quantities of light machine guns, used not as machine guns, but as automatic rifles, snipers' tools, by men kept deliberately in ignorance of their mechanism, so that the speed of action would not be hampered by attempts at repair. If a gun jammed, the gunner had to throw it away and go on with his rifle. We made another special feature of high explosives, and nearly every one in the revolt was qualified by rule of thumb experience in demolition work. We invented special methods of our own, for rapid work under fire, in the course of our months of practice, and before the end were dealing with any quantity of track and bridges economically and safely.

On some occasions we strengthened tribal raids

by armoured cars, manned by Englishmen. Armoured cars, once they have found a possible track, can keep up with a camel party. They are, however, cumbrous and shorter-ranged, because of the difficulty of carrying petrol. Therefore we seldom used them more than a hundred miles from home. On the march to Damascus, when we were nearly four hundred miles off our base, we first maintained them by a baggage train of petrol-laden camels, and afterwards by the help of the Air Force were able to give them further supplies by Handley-Page. Cars are magnificent fighting machines, and decisive whenever they can come into action on their own conditions. But though each has for main principle that of "fire in movement," yet the tactical employments of cars and camel-corps are so different that I do not recommend their being used in joint operations, except in very special circumstances. We found it demoralising to both to use armoured and unarmoured cavalry together.

The distribution of the raiding parties was unorthodox. It was impossible to mix or combine tribes, since they disliked or distrusted one another. Likewise we could not use the men of one tribe in the territory of another. In consequence, we aimed at the widest distribution of forces; in order to have the greatest number of raids on hand at once, and we added fluidity to their ordinary speed by using one district on Monday, another on Tuesday, a third on Wednesday. This much reinforced their natural mobility. It gave us priceless advantages in pursuit, for the force renewed itself with fresh men in every new tribal area, and gave us always our pristine energy. Maximum disorder was in a real sense our equilibrium.

The internal economy of the raiding parties was equally curious. We aimed at maximum articulation. We were serving a common ideal, without tribal emulation, and so we could not hope for any *esprit de corps* to reinforce our motives. Soldiers are made a caste either by being given great pay and rewards in money, uniform, or political privileges; or, as in England, by being made outcasts, cut off from their fellows by contempt. We could not knit man to man, for our tribesmen were in arms willingly, by conviction. There have been many armies enlisted voluntarily: there have been few armies serving voluntarily under such trying conditions, for so long a war as ours. Any of the Arabs could go home whenever the conviction failed him. Our only contract was honour.

Consequently we had no discipline, in the sense in which it is restrictive, submergent of individuality, the lowest common denominator of men. In regular armies in peace it means the limit of energy attainable by everybody present: it is the hunt not of an average, but of an absolute, a 100-per-cent. standard, in which the ninety-nine stronger men are played down to the level of the worst. The aim is to render the unit a unit, and the man a type, in order that their effort shall be calculable, their collective output even in grain and in bulk. The deeper the discipline, the lower the individual efficiency, and the more sure the performance. It is a deliberate sacrifice of capacity in order to reduce the uncertain element, the bionomic factor, in enlisted humanity, and its accompaniment is *compound* or social war, that form in which the man in the fighting line has to be the product of the multiplied exertions of the long hierarchy, from workshop to supply unit, which maintains him in the field.

The Arab war was *simple* and individual. Every enrolled man served in the line of battle, and was self-contained. We had no lines of communication or labour troops. The efficiency of each man was his personal efficiency. We thought that in our condition of warfare the sum yielded by single men would be at least equal to the product of a compound system, and it was certainly easier to adjust to tribal life and manners, given elasticity and understanding on the part of the commanding officers. Fortunately for our chances nearly every young Englishman has the roots of eccentricity in him, and so we got on well enough. Of course we used very few Englishmen in the field, not more than one per thousand of the Arab troops. A larger proportion would have created friction, just because they were foreign bodies (pearls if you please) in the oyster: and those who were present controlled by influence and advice, by their superior knowledge, not by an extraneous authority.

In practice we did not employ in the firing line the greater numbers which the adoption of a "simple" system put theoretically at our disposal. We preferred to use them in relay: otherwise our attack would have become too extended. Each man had to have liberal work-room. In irregular war if two men are together one is being wasted. The moral strain of isolated action makes this simple form of war very exacting on the individual soldier, and demands from him special initiative, endurance and enthusiasm. Our ideal was to make action a series of single combats. Napoleon, in his pregnant valuation of the Mamelukes in terms of French soldiers, first gave me the idea: Ardant du Picq widened its application: the prejudices of historians are generally the richest part of their histories. Our value depended entirely on our quality, not on our quantity. We had to keep always cool, for the excitement of a blood-lust would impair the science of our combatants, and our victory depended on our just use of speed, concealment, accuracy of fire. Irregular war is far more intellectual than a bayonet charge.

The illiteracy of our forces was not harmful, since we worked intentionally in these small numbers and explained our plan verbally to every one. Their very illiteracy has trained them to a longer memory and a closer hearing of the news. Nor were our tactics too subtle, for they had to be translated into independent action through the heads of our followers, and success was impossible unless most of them used their intelligence to forward our conception against the moral and material accidents of the path. This dilution of tactical ability to the level of the lowest interpreter was regrettable, but not all loss. The only alternative would be independent enterprise, and a mediocre design, persisted in, is grander than a series of brilliant expedients and will overcome them in the end.

By careful persistence, kept strictly within our strength and following the spirit of our theories, we were able eventually to reduce the Turks to helplessness, and complete victory seemed to be almost within our sight when General Allenby by his immense stroke in Palestine threw the enemy's main forces into hopeless confusion and put an immediate end to the Turkish war. We were very happy to have done with all our pains, but sometimes since I have felt a private regret that his too-greatness deprived me of the opportunity of following to the end the dictum of Saxe that a war might be won without fighting battles. It was an irony of fate to entrust this side-show of a side-show, with its opportunity of proving or disproving the theory, to an outsider like myself, not qualified technically to make the best of it. I would have given so much to show that Saxe was the greatest master of his kind of war, but now all I can say is that we worked by his light for two years, and the work stood. This is a pragmatic argument that cannot be wholly derided.

Unfortunately our campaigns lacked a historian as much as an executant. Now that I try to write down what we did, and why, some of our principles look truisms (mankind would so rather believe a sophism) and some look contradictory. The fault must be either in my exposition or in my observation. Savage warfare seems never to have been thought out in English from the savage point of view, and the Arab revolt would have been a great opportunity for a thinker to test its possibilities on a grand scale. Our war was so odd and so far away that coy Authority left us to ourselves. We had no base machinery, no formal staff, no clerks, no government, no telegraphs, no public opinion, no troops of British nationality, no honour, no conventions. The experiment was a thrilling one, which took all our wits. We believed we would prove irregular war or rebellion to be an exact science, and an inevitable success, granted certain factors and if pursued along certain lines. We did not prove it, because the war stopped: but here the thesis is:—

It seemed that rebellion must have an unassailable base, something guarded not merely from attack, but from the fear of it: such a base as we had in the Red Sea Ports, the desert, or in the minds of the men we converted to our creed. It must have a sophisticated alien enemy, in the form of a disciplined army of occupation too small to fulfil the doctrine of acreage: too few to adjust number to space, in order to dominate the whole area effectively from fortified posts. It must have a friendly population, not actively friendly, but sympathetic to the point of not betraying rebel movements to the enemy. Rebellions can be made by 2 per cent. active in a striking force, and 98 per cent. passively sympathetic. The few active rebels must have the qualities of speed and endurance, ubiquity and independence of arteries of supply. They must have the technical equipment to destroy or paralyse the enemy's organised communications, for irregular war is fairly Willisen's definition of strategy, "the study of communication" in its extreme degree, of attack where the enemy is not. In fifty words: Granted mobility, security (in the form of denying targets to the enemy), time, and doctrine (the idea to convert every subject to friendliness), victory will rest with the insurgents, for the algebraical factors are in the end decisive, and against them perfections of means and spirit struggle quite in vain.

IV

THE
SUPPRESSED INTRODUCTORY
CHAPTER FOR *SEVEN PILLARS
OF WISDOM*

EDITOR'S NOTE

THE subscribers' edition of *Seven Pillars of Wisdom* contains no Chapter XI, for the original first chapter had been omitted in the course of proof correction, and renumbering proceeded only as far as the next ten. The omitted chapter was suppressed at that time on the advice of Mr Bernard Shaw, and for political reasons has not since been published, apart from a couple of paragraphs quoted from the "Oxford" unrevised text, which reproduces the manuscript (David Garnett, *Letters of T. E. Lawrence*, p. 262).

The present version is that found among the proof sheets of the subscribers' edition.

The author's views on Mesopotamia are perhaps coloured by post-War developments. The objectives intended to be secured by the expeditionary force were more complex and less sordid than is commonly believed.

The country's value as a source of food was then overrated, but usable oil had not yet been produced in Iraq and none could have been exported because of difficulties of transport;

on the other hand, it was important to safeguard the Persian oilfield at the head of the Gulf and to prevent the establishment of a German submarine-base there. (Summaries of official documents of the time may be found in *Iraq*, an authoritative study by the American scholar, Philip Ireland.)

A. W. L.

THE SUPPRESSED INTRODUCTORY CHAPTER FOR *SEVEN PILLARS OF WISDOM*

THE story which follows was first written out in *Design of* Paris during the Peace Conference, from notes *the Story* jotted daily on the march, strengthened by some reports sent to my chiefs in Cairo. Afterwards, in the autumn of 1919, this first draft and some of the notes were lost. It seemed to me historically needful to reproduce the tale, as perhaps no one but myself in Feisal's army had thought of writing down at the time what we felt, what we hoped, what we tried. So it was built again with heavy repugnance in London in the winter of 1919–20 from memory and my surviving notes. The record of events was not dulled in me and perhaps few actual mistakes crept in—except in details of dates or numbers—but the outlines and significance of things had lost edge in the haze of new interests.

Dates and places are correct, so far as my notes preserved them: but the personal names are not. Since the adventure some of those who worked with me have buried themselves in the shallow grave of public duty. Free use has been made of their names. Others still possess themselves, and here keep their secrecy. Sometimes one man carries various names. This may hide individuality and make the book a scatter of featureless puppets, rather than a group of living people: but once good is told of a man, and again evil, and some would not thank me for either blame or praise.

This isolated picture throwing the main light upon myself is unfair to my British colleagues. Especially I am most sorry that I have not told what the non-commissioned of us did. They were inarticulate, but wonderful, especially when it is taken into account that they had not the motive, the imaginative vision of the end, which sustained the officers. Unfortunately my concern was limited to this end, and the book is just a designed procession of Arab freedom from Mecca to Damascus. It is intended to rationalise the

Fellow-ship of Revolt

campaign, that everyone may see how natural the success was and how inevitable, how little dependent on direction or brain, how much less on the outside assistance of the few British. It was an Arab war waged and led by Arabs for an Arab aim in Arabia.

My proper share was a minor one, but because of a fluent pen, a free speech, and a certain adroitness of brain, I took upon myself, as I describe it, a mock primacy. In reality I never had any office among the Arabs: was never in charge of the British mission with them. Wilson, Joyce, Newcombe, Dawnay, and Davenport were all over my head. I flattered myself that I was too young, not that they had more heart or mind in the work. I did my best. Wilson, Newcombe, Joyce, Dawnay, Davenport, Buxton, Marshall, Stirling, Young, Maynard, Ross, Scott, Winterton, Lloyd, Wordie, Siddons, Goslett, Stent, Henderson, Spence, Gilman, Garland, Brodie, Makins, Nunan, Leeson, Hornby, Peake, Scott-Higgins, Ramsay, Wood, Hinde, Bright, Macindoe, Greenhill, Grisenthwaite, Dowsett, Bennett, Wade, Gray, Pascoe and the others also did their best.

It would be impertinent in me to praise them. When I wish to say ill of one outside our number, I do it: though there is less of this than was in my diary, since the passage of time seems to have bleached out men's stains. When I wish to praise outsiders, I do it: but our family affairs are our own. We did what we set out to do, and have the satisfaction of that knowledge. The others have liberty some day to put on record their story, one parallel to mine but not mentioning more of me than I of them, for each of us did his job by himself and as he pleased, hardly seeing his friends.

In these pages the history is not of the Arab movement, but of me in it. It is a narrative of daily life, mean happenings, little people. Here are no lessons for the world, no disclosures to shock peoples. It is filled with trivial things, partly that no one mistake for history the bones from which some day a man may make history, and partly for the pleasure it gave me to recall the fellowship of the revolt. We were fond together, because of the sweep of the open places, the taste of wide winds, the sunlight, and the hopes in which we worked. The morning freshness of the world-to-be intoxicated us. We were wrought up with ideas inexpressible and vaporous, but to be fought for. We lived many lives in those whirling campaigns, never sparing ourselves: yet when we achieved and the new world dawned, the old men came out again and took our victory to re-make in the likeness of the former world they knew. Youth could win, but had not learned to keep: and was pitiably weak against age. We stammered that we had worked for a new heaven and a new earth, and they thanked us kindly and made their peace.

All men dream: but not equally. Those who dream by night in the dusty recesses of their minds wake in the day to find that it was vanity: but the dreamers of the day are dangerous men, for they may act their dream with open eyes, to make it possible. This I did. I meant to make a new nation, to restore a lost influence, to give twenty millions of Semites the foundation on which to build an inspired dream-palace of their national thoughts. So high an aim called out the inherent nobility of their minds, and made them play a generous part in events: but when we won, it was charged against me that the British petrol royalties in Mesopotamia were become dubious, and French Colonial policy ruined in the Levant. *Youth: Age: and Dreams*

I am afraid that I hope so. We pay for these things too much in honour and in innocent lives. I went up the Tigris with one hundred Devon Territorials, young, clean, delightful fellows, full of the power of happiness and of making women and children glad. By them one saw vividly how great it was to be their kin, and English. And we were casting them by thousands into the fire to the worst of deaths, not to win the war but that the corn and rice and oil of Mesopotamia might be ours. The only need was to defeat our enemies (Turkey among them), and this was at last done in the wisdom of Allenby with less than four hundred killed, by turning to our uses the hands of the oppressed in Turkey. I am proudest of my thirty fights in that I did not have any of our own blood shed. All our subject provinces to me were not worth one dead Englishman.

We were three years over this effort and I have had to hold back many things which may not yet be said. Even so, parts of this book will be new to nearly all who see it, and many will look for familiar things and not find them. Once I reported fully to my chiefs, but learnt that they were rewarding me on my own evidence. This was not as it should be. Honours may be necessary in a professional army, as so many emphatic mentions in despatches, and by enlisting we had put ourselves, willingly or not, in the position of regular soldiers.

Con-
spiracy
and
Fraud
For my work on the Arab front I had determined to accept nothing. The Cabinet raised the Arabs to fight for us by definite promises of self-government afterwards. Arabs believe in persons, not in institutions. They saw in me a free agent of the British Government, and demanded from me an endorsement of its written

promises. So I had to join the conspiracy, and, for what my word was worth, assured the men of their reward. In our two years' partnership under fire they grew accustomed to believing me and to think my Government, like myself, sincere. In this hope they performed some fine things, but, of course, instead of being proud of what we did together, I was continually and bitterly ashamed.

It was evident from the beginning that if we won the war these promises would be dead paper, and had I been an honest adviser of the Arabs I would have advised them to go home and not risk their lives fighting for such stuff: but I salved myself with the hope that, by leading these Arabs madly in the final victory I would establish them, with arms in their hands, in a position so assured (if not dominant) that expediency would counsel to the Great Powers a fair settlement of their claims. In other words, I presumed (seeing no other leader with the will and power) that I would survive the campaigns, and be able to defeat not merely the Turks on the battlefield, but my own country and its allies in the council-chamber. It was an immodest presumption: it is not yet clear if I succeeded: but it is clear that I had no shadow of leave to engage the Arabs, unknowing, in such hazard. I risked the fraud, on my conviction that Arab help was necessary to our cheap and speedy victory in the East, and that better we win and break our word than lose.

The dismissal of Sir Henry McMahon confirmed my belief in our essential insincerity: but I could not so explain myself to General Wingate while the war lasted, since I was nominally under his orders, and he did not seem sensible of how false his own standing was. The only thing remaining was to refuse rewards for being a successful trickster and, to prevent this unpleasantness arising, I began in my reports to conceal the true stories of things, and to persuade the few Arabs who knew to an equal reticence. In this book also, for the last time, I mean to be my own judge of what to say.

V
ON
ERIC KENNINGTON'S
ARAB PORTRAITS

EDITOR'S NOTE

In February 1927 the Leicester Galleries, London, issued the "Catalogue of an Exhibition of Paintings, Pastels, Drawings and Woodcuts, illustrating Col. T. E. Lawrence's book, *Seven Pillars of Wisdom*, with Prefaces by Bernard Shaw and T. E. Lawrence." The first preface has already been reprinted (with minor alterations) as part of the article by Bernard Shaw in *T. E. Lawrence by his Friends*. The other, written long before, was devoted to Eric Kennington's drawings of Arabs, in the expectation that they would be shown as a special exhibition. The manuscript was sent from Aden on 25th August 1921. Its opening sentence was altered by Mr Kennington to read "one of these" instead of "some of these," for accuracy's sake, but the portrait in question represented an English official. Further comments made by T. E. Lawrence when he saw the portraits are quoted in Mr Kennington's article in *T. E. Lawrence by his Friends*.

The text is now reprinted without the

Catalogue's reference numbers. In their place are given page references to *Seven Pillars of Wisdom*, Jonathan Cape's edition, where the drawings are reproduced.

A. W. L.

ON ERIC KENNINGTON'S
ARAB PORTRAITS

I saw him doing one of these and can testify that he did not know why he was working, nor how he was working. When he felt that he knew things went very badly. When he began to whistle softly, things were moving well; and as some Arabs think that whistling is a speech with devils, many of his subjects must have felt themselves in bad company before their sittings ended. He was drawing odd people, who are very impatient of those they think fools, men without ties, or duties, or claims, rank individualists who cling to their barren country that they may owe nothing to any man, and be owed nothing in return. Very difficult sitters they are.

It was a strange chance which put him in contact with this society, but he rose to his occasion and brought a full selection of his opportunities back with him in his portfolio.

He has drawn camel-men, and princes of the desert, donkey-boys, officers, descendants of the Prophet, a vice-president of the Turkish Chamber, slaves, sheikhs and swordsmen. They represent a fair choice of the real Arab, not the Algerian or Egyptian or Syrian so commonly palmed off on us, not the noisy, luxury-loving, sensual, passionate, greedy person, but a man whose ruling characteristic is hardness, of body, mind, heart, and head.

This is no doubt where my being asked to write a note comes in, for I know these odd people who sat to him, and some of them have been my friends. The causes of his going out to Arabia were, a poet, something a man said, and an unpublished book of mine. His Arabs were amongst those who fought gallantly for their freedom in the War. Freedom is a profane, not a saintly body, for which they cared too exclusively to have spare mind to see themselves in action. It never occurred to them that their children might want to know what they did, and so they wrote down nothing of their story. I felt that this was a mistake, and set about making loose notes in the leisure and detachment which I had, for our race has been free so long that by now we have forgotten that first wonderful taste; indeed age has made it cloying, and sometimes we wish for chains as a variety.

This book was something for the future, but

it was an outside view, from an odd angle, and words, especially an amateur's words, are unsatisfactory to describe persons. It seemed to us that it would be balanced somewhat by an expert view, from another angle: and so Kennington went out to correct my men. He was to have had me as his guide, but circumstances prevented this, and plunged him alone into a great Arab camp, which was in a state of semi-warfare. There he had nothing better than a bell-tent for working in, and an atmosphere of unrest and uncertainty which made work difficult.

I had meant to help him in his selection of subjects to draw: as events turned out he was thrown on his own judgment. It is interesting to see that instinctively he drew the men of the desert. Where he was there were ten settled men to every nomad: yet his drawings show nearly ten desert men to every peasant. This has strengthened in me the unflattering suspicion that the nomad is the richer creature.

The Arab townsman or villager is like us and our villagers, with our notion of property, our sense of gain and our appetite for material success. He has our premises as well as our processes. The Beduin, on the other hand, while his sense is as human and his mind as logical as ours, begins with principles quite other than our own, and gets further from us as his character strengthens. He has a creed and practice of not-possessing, which is a tough armour against our modern wiles. It defends him against all sentiment.

Somehow or other Kennington persuaded them to sit; and when he came home, and turned over his sheets of paper in front of me, the experience was very wonderful. I saw first one and then another of the men whom I had known, and at once learned to know them better. This may point indirectly to the power of the drawings as works of art: it pointed without contest to their literary completeness as illustrations of my memory of the men in action: and I think it is praise of psychology. There is quite admirable character here.

Some are curiously typical. Of course they are individual enough, speaking portraits of the men in many of their moods and attitudes: but often Kennington has reached behind the particular, and made them also types. Perhaps it was because of the language bar, which forced him to rely entirely on his visual powers. However it is, in this study and in that you see not only So and So, son of So and So, but a representation of all the Ageyl who ever rode out from

Bagdad, or of all the freedom of the palm-oases of Nejd. In his Sherifs and in his Sheikhs you see the spirit of the race of sherifs, or of the class of sheikhs sitting within these men's clothes, inhabiting their features, giving a broader significance to their shapes. These drawings are deep and sharp renderings of all that Western Arabians are.

They are quite literal, not prettied or idealised in any way. Yet it would not be fair to call them average. Kennington chose some of the finest men within his reach for his sitters. Auda abu Tayi (p. 222) is the best man in Arabia to have beside you in a fight: you are good enough if you can keep near him for long. He is a mosaic of quixotic splendours: and when he dies the "Middle Ages" of the desert will have ended. Said el Sikeini (p. 378) is a dour puritan, who saw his men dragging chests of gold and rich merchandise from the train which he had blown up by a mine. He left them plundering while he carefully rolled up and carried away the wire and electrical gear with which he had fired this mine, and with which he meant to fire the next. There is Sherif Shakir (p. 198), the finest horseman in Arabia, and one of its bravest and richest and most beloved men. There is the boy Mahmas

(p. 292) whom our standards would make a murderer. He is short-tempered and proud, and cannot endure to be worsted in argument. When it happens he leans forward with his little knife and kills the other party. Three times he did it before people learnt to respect his convictions, however ill-expressed. His elder brother, a responsible parent, each time saved him from odium by discharging on the nail the blood-money which heals the dispute and compensates the bereaved. There is the Emir Abdulla (p. 68) who will read this note, and would not thank me for either praise or blame of him. His complexity comes out in this portrait.

At the other end of the scale is the spy (p. 260) who was our most excellent informant in the War, but is looked down upon by his fellows because he took money for his work. He lost the money in a bad trading venture after the armistice, and now without either friends or substance must serve as a donkey-boy where he once walked free. His face shows his sense of the broken world about him: but when he was sent for to be drawn he ran home and put on his best clothing. It was not very good, but evidently he still has hope and self-respect.

Ali ibn Hussein, Fahad, Matar, Mohammad

ARAB PORTRAITS

Sheri, Sindah: the desert is full of songs and legends of their fighting, books could be written round them by the Arabs, and personally I am very content to have had a share in causing to be made these records of their faces while the knowledge of what they did is fresh in men's minds. Whoever writes those books will have to write well if he is to do honour to his illustrations.

VI
THE WAR
PHOTOGRAPHS

EDITOR'S NOTE

DURING and after the War, T. E. Lawrence formed a large collection of his own negatives and prints of other people's photographs to illustrate the Arab revolt. A selection now belongs to the Imperial War Museum, having been presented by him or by Captain B. H. Liddell Hart. None of these is reproduced here, for they can be consulted and prints obtained at the Museum. The negatives retained in private possession have begun to decay, and it has therefore been thought advisable to publish all which can be possibly considered fit for reproduction. Their quality seems to have often been poor from the start, partly because the glaring light in which many were taken concealed minor inequalities in the surface of objects or landscapes, partly because the films deteriorated rapidly in the great heat during the weeks or months which passed before they could be developed. But apart from historical associations, some of these photographs possess a peculiar value as representations of country which otherwise has never been photographed, and of the mode of life which was exacted by the physical environment and is now ceasing to exist.

The prints in the War Museum and in the personal collection were labelled by T. E. Lawrence and others; and the descriptions in this book are based on those identifications, but the spellings of Arabic names have been brought into conformity with the index of *Seven Pillars of Wisdom*.

The photographs are arranged as far as possible in the order in which the subjects are mentioned in *Seven Pillars of Wisdom*.

A. W. L.

ALPHABETICAL INDEX OF *PERSONS*
AND PLACES SHOWN IN THE
WAR PHOTOGRAPHS

Plate I

NAKHL MUBARAK from the South

Plate 1

Plate 2

Gardens of Nakhl Mubarak with Abd el Kerim el Beidawi in foreground

Plate 2

169

Plate 3

NAKHL MUBARAK

Plate 4

NAKHL MUBARAK

Plate 3

Plate 4

Plate 5

The Spring at NAKHL MUBARAK

Plate 6

NAKHL MUBARAK looking on to Jebel AGIDA

Plate 5

Plate 6

Plate 7

From NAKHL MUBARAK looking up Wadi YENBO towards
KHEIF HUSSEIN

Plate 8

NAKHL MUBARAK in middle distance, RUDHWA in background

Plate 7

Plate 8

175

Plate 9

Looking from the hills behind the rock ground across
NAKHL MUBARAK groves up Wadi YENBO

Plate 10

NAKHL MUBARAK, edge of landing ground

Plate 9

Plate 10

Plate 11

Maulud el Mukhlus and the Mule M.I. with Meccan Infantry at Nakhl Mubarak, Rudhwa in background, December 1916

Plate 11

179

Plate 12

Outside the Emir FEISAL'S Tent at NAKHL MUBARAK landing ground

Plate 13

Dawn in Camp, NAKHL MUBARAK, December 1916

Plate 12

Plate 13

181   M

Plate 14

Nebk

Plate 15

From a Mound in Wadi Yenbo. Hill in distance and centre is Jel
Anagein, the double-peaked summit of Jebel Figra. The brus
ground flat is Wadi Yenbo

Plate 14

Plate 15

Plate 16

From Nakhl Mubarak, Jeria on extreme left, Wadi Yenbo in centre and right

Plate 16

185

Plate 17

From NAKHL MUBARAK, JERIA extreme right, RUDHWA in background

Plate 18

Looking over BIR EL FAGIR from a hill North-West of NAKHL MUBARA
Jebel FIJER on right in distance. In centre distance Jebel DHIFR.
and the hill range bounding Wadi SAFRA on West. Middle distan
BRUKA

Plate 17

Plate 18

187

Plate 19

Background on left, BRUKA on its mound; middle distance NAKHL MUBARAK
looking South.   FEISAL in black cloak, foreground centre

Plate 20

The Mejlis outside FEISAL's Tent at NAKHL MUBARAK

Plate 19

Plate 20

189

Plate 21

Plate 22

Feisal's Army coming in to Yenbo, December 1916

Plate 21

Plate 22

Plate 23

FEISAL's Army coming in to YENBO, December 1916

Plate 24

YENBO

Plate 25

YENBO

Plate 24

Plate 25

Plate 26

Yenbo—T. E. Lawrence's house on right

Plate 27

House at Yenbo

Plate 26

Plate 27

Plate 28

Yenbo—Sheikh Abd el Kader el Abdo, and Staff

Plate 29

Yenbo—Abd el Kader el Abdo

Plate 28

Plate 29

Plate 30

WEJH looking East

Plate 31

EL NIJL—SHOBEK Railway and Mill

Plate 30

Plate 31

Plate 32
Arab Camp at WEJH

Plate 32

Plate 33

Emir Feisal and Sherif Sharraf leading the Ageyl Bodyguard Northwards on the first stage to Wejh, January 1917

Plate 33

Plate 34

FEISAL and AGEYL Bodyguard

Plate 35

FEISAL and AGEYL Bodyguard

Plate 34

Plate 35

Plate 36
AGEYL Bodyguard

Plate 37
AGEYL Bodyguard

Plate 36

Plate 37

Plate 38

AGEYL Bodyguard

Plate 39

AGEYL Bodyguard

Plate 38

Plate 39

Plate 40

AGEYL Bodyguard

Plate 41

AGEYL Bodyguard

Plate 40

Plate 41

Plate 42
Um Lejj

Plate 43
Um Lejj

Plate 42

Plate 43

215

Plate 44

Behind Um Lejj

Plate 45

Semna, Col. Newcombe in Palm Trees

Plate 44

Plate 45

217

Plate 46
Jebel EL SUKHUR

Plate 46

Plate 47
Jebel EL SUKHUR

Plate 48
Jebel EL SUKHUR

Plate 47

Plate 48

Plate 49

Salt Pool in Wadi HAMDH near EL UGILA

Plate 50

BRUKA Irrigation Channel

Plate 49

Plate 50

223

Plate 51

In Wadi HAMDH near SUEJJ

Plate 52

Wadi HAMDH with Jebel RAAL to the East, from ABU ZEREIBAT

Plate 51

Plate 52

Plate 53
Jebel Raal

Plate 53

Plate 54
Jebel Raal

Plate 55
El Hesna

Plate 54

Plate 55

229

P

Plate 56

ABU ZEREIBAT Water Pool

Plate 57

ABU ZEREIBAT

Plate 56

Plate 57

Plate 58

Entering Wadi WAHEIDA

Plate 59

Jebel SHEMEL

Plate 58

Plate 59

Plate 60

FEISAL'S Army coming in to WEJH, January 1917

Plate 60

235

Plate 61
Sherif Nasir

Plate 62
Dakh el Allah el Ghair

Plate 61

Plate 62

237

Plate 63

<small>Auda abu Tayi</small>

Plate 64

<small>Auda abu Tayi</small> and his Kinsmen on the first day of the march from
<small>Wejh</small> to the <small>Howeitat</small> in their spring pastures of the Syrian Desert,
May 1917

Plate 63

Plate 64

239

Plate 65
Wadi KITAN

Plate 66
Wadi HANBAG

Plate 65

Plate 66

Plate 67

Wadi GARA

Plate 68

Wadi GARA

Plate 67

Plate 68

Plate 69

Wadi Murrmiya

Plate 70

Harrat el Gara—Wadi Murrmiya

Plate 69

Plate 70

Plate 71

Behind Wadi Gara and Wadi Murrmiya

Plate 72

Crater at Ras Gara

Plate 71

Plate 72

Plate 73

ABU MARKHA

Plate 74

ABU MARKHA—ABDULLA'S Tents

Plate 73

Plate 74

Plate 75

ABU MARKHA Well

Plate 76

Wadi AIS at ABU MARKHA

Plate 75

Plate 76

251

Plate 77

Sherif SHAKIR

Plate 78

MOHAMMED EL KADHI

Plate 77

Plate 78

Plate 79

GHADIR OSMAN, on the return journey from AIS to WEJH

Plate 79

Plate 80

Wadi Arnoua

Plate 81

Khauthila—Bir ibn Rifada

Plate 80

Plate 81

Plate 82

KALAAT SEBEIL at WEJH.   The party the day before starting for the
SIRHAN, 9th May 1917

Plate 83

KALAAT SEBEIL, 9th May 1917

Plate 82

Plate 83

Plate 84
EL KURR

Plate 84

261   R

Plate 85

EL KURR

Plate 86

RUBIAAN WELL

Plate 85

Plate 86

263

Plate 87

ABU RAGA (on the way to the SIRHAN, May 1917)

Plate 88

ABU RAGA

Plate 87

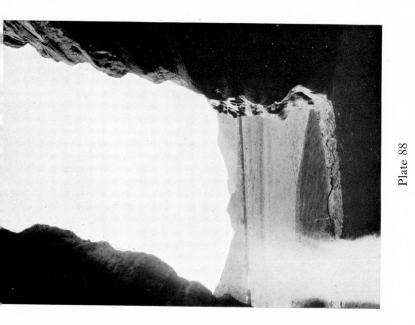

Plate 88

265

Plate 89

Sheikh ZAAL IBN MOTLOG

Plate 90

DHAIF ALLAH IBN HOMEID, HUSHON and Servant

Plate 89

Plate 90

Plate 91
EL SHEGG

Plate 92
EL SHEGG

Plate 91

Plate 92

269

Plate 93
Unidentified

Plate 94
Unidentified

Plate 93

Plate 94

271

Plate 95

Guweira Plain

Plate 96

Guweira

Plate 95

Plate 96

Plate 97

Wadi SIRHAN

Plate 98

The approach on AKABA during a sandstorm, July 1917

Plate 97

Plate 98

Plate 99

In Wadi Itm near RESAFE while discussing terms of Turkish surrender, July 5th, 1917

Plate 99

277   S

Plate 100

EL HESNA in the GAAT EL RUMM

Plate 101

RUMM

Plate 100

Plate 101

Plate 102
TAFILEH, January 1918

Plate 102

281

Plate 103

TAFILEH, Turkish prisoners defiling

Plate 103

283

Plate 104

ZEID, ABDULLA, RASIM and LUFTI, with captured Austrian Guns
at TAFILEH

Plate 105

TAFILEH, captured Machine Guns

Plate 104

Plate 105

Plate 106
MAHMAS IBN DAKHIL

Plate 107
A SHEIKH

Plate 106

Plate 107

Plate 108

KHARANEH

Plate 109

KHARANEH

Plate 108

Plate 109

Plate 110
AZRAK

Plate 111
AZRAK

Plate 110

Plate 111